# The Value of Virginia Woolf

In *The Value of Virgini̇ ̇ ̇ ̇* ̇ ̇ ̇ ̇ings of Virginia
Woolf, from her early ̇ ̇ ̇ ̇ ̇. Detloff
demonstrates why Woo ̇ ̇ ̇ ̇ as a defender of
modernist experimenta ̇ ̇ ̇ ̇ ic vision who
also exhibits moments ̇ ̇ ̇ ̇ famously
enigmatic figure, Woolf ̇ ̇ ̇ ̇ ewards to
different readers. *The Vȧ ̇ ̇ ̇* ̇ ̇ ̇not only the significance of
her most celebrated fictiȯ ̇, but also the interplay of precision and freedom, beauty
and wit, voice and language that give Woolf's writings their perennial appeal.

**Madelyn Detloff** is Associate Professor of English and Women's, Gender, and
Sexuality Studies at Miami University. She is the author of *The Persistence of
Modernism: Loss and Mourning in the Twentieth Century* and has published
widely in such journals as *Hypatia, Women's Studies: An Interdisciplinary Journal,
ELN, Literature Compass,* the MLA *Approaches to Teaching* series, and
*Modernism/Modernity.*

# The Value of Virginia Woolf

Madelyn Detloff
*Miami University*

# CAMBRIDGE
## UNIVERSITY PRESS

32 Avenue of the Americas, New York, NY 10013-2473, USA

Cambridge University Press is part of the University of Cambridge.

It furthers the University's mission by disseminating knowledge in the pursuit of education, learning, and research at the highest international levels of excellence.

www.cambridge.org
Information on this title: www.cambridge.org/9781107441514

© Madelyn Detloff 2016

First published 2016

Printed in the United Kingdom by Clays, St Ives plc

*A catalog record for this publication is available from the British Library.*

*Library of Congress Cataloging in Publication Data*
Detloff, Madelyn, 1965– author.
The value of Virginia Woolf / Madelyn Detloff.
New York : Cambridge University Press, 2016. | Includes bibliographical references and index.
LCCN 2015040732 | ISBN 9781107081505 (hardback)
LCSH: Woolf, Virginia, 1882–1941 – Criticism and interpretation. | BISAC: LITERARY CRITICISM / Women Authors.
LCC PR6045.O72 Z6135 2016 | DDC 823/.912–dc23
LC record available at http://lccn.loc.gov/2015040732

ISBN 978-1-107-08150-5 Hardback
ISBN 978-1-107-44151-4 Paperback

# Contents

# Acknowledgments

Portions of the Introduction, now revised, appear in *Writing the World: Selected Papers from the Twenty-Fourth Annual Conference on Virginia Woolf*, edited by Diana Swanson and Pamela Caughie (Clemson: Clemson University Press, 2015).

Portions of Chapter 3, now revised, appear in *Interdisciplinary/ Multidisciplinary Woolf: Selected Papers from the Twenty-Second Annual International Conference on Virginia Woolf*, edited by Ann Martin and Kathryn Holland (Clemson: Clemson University Digital Press, 2013).

My profound gratitude to Laura Holliday for her extraordinary editing; to my current and former students, who have taught me more than I have taught them; to my colleagues, especially my writing group compatriots Mary Jean Corbett, Katie Johnson, Tim Melley, Elisabeth Hodges, and Peggy Shaffer; to the members of the International Virginia Woolf Society; to my editor Ray Ryan and the outstanding external reviewers for Cambridge University Press; and to Gaile Pohlhaus, Jr., for her tutelage in the finer points of Plato, Aristotle, and Wittgenstein, as well as for her support and insight throughout this project.

# Introduction
# On Value

One cannot speak of value without implicitly or explicitly speaking of values. Barbara Herrnstein Smith made this point eloquently clear in her meticulous study of the "double discourse" of value, *Contingencies of Value*.[1] "On the one hand," Smith explains, "there is the discourse of economic theory: money, commerce, technology, industry, production and consumption, workers and consumers; on the other hand, there is the discourse of aesthetic axiology: culture, art, genius, creation and appreciation, artists and connoisseurs."[2] These two "hands" may use different yardsticks for measuring what is worth one's time, money, effort, or attention, but both participate in the same complex, dynamic system of evaluation – a system that is social and interdependent, rather than presocial or transcendent. Arguing that "All value is radically contingent, being neither a fixed attribute, an inherent quality, or an objective property of things but, rather, an effect of multiple, continuously changing, and continuously interacting variables," Smith eschews the notion of intrinsic aesthetic value (a value that inheres in things, in works), and claims, rather, that value is conferred through communal processes – that is, through the *work* of valuing.[3]

This work goes unnoticed when there is a high degree of agreement in a community. When there is less consensus in a community about particular practices, inclinations, or forms, cultural artifacts that align with those practices, inclinations, or forms will be regarded as matters of personal preference: some people prefer Beethoven to Bach, Beyoncé to Taylor Swift, blue to green.[4] When there is general agreement in a community – say, that Beethoven's music is worthy of more regard than Taylor Swift's, or that a Michelangelo fresco is worth preserving while a spray-painted wall in Los Angeles can (and, some would say, should) be targeted for removal – the preference for Beethoven or Michelangelo will seem to be intrinsic to the music or the painting, rather than the result of unacknowledged, perhaps unconscious, communal decision-making. For Smith, "Here, as elsewhere, *a co-incidence of contingencies among individual subjects who interact as members of some community will operate for them as noncontingency and be interpreted by them accordingly.*"[5] To claim that value is contingent is not to say is that all things are equal – Bansky=Beethoven=Beyoncé – but rather to acknowledge that aesthetic value operates much more like exchange value than many of us would like to admit, accruing over years, even millennia, through "complex interrelations among human needs, technological production, and cultural practices" that are recursively reinforced, according to Smith, through "a continuous process of mutual modification between our desires and our universe."[6] In other words, cultural capital begets cultural capital in much the same way that capital begets more capital.

This knowledge can make one regard cynically any claim about the value of the work of a particular author, artist, or composer, but only if the social, interdependent aspect of valuing is seen as debasing or corrupting. We could, instead, consider the contingency of aesthetic value as a powerful heuristic for illuminating a culture's ideals, unspoken preferences (for better or worse), and hierarchies of worth. These preferences, ideals, and hierarchies are, unlike allegedly transcendent measures of value, open to reflection, contestation, and recursive remaking. Melba Cuddy-Keane highlights the generative potential of Smith's dynamic theory of value, arguing that Smith's theory "takes us beyond confrontations of differing values to an analysis of the way value operates by alerting us both to the institutional production of value and to the 'countermechanisms' within the community for challenging, contradicting, and subverting normative claims."[7] The history of Woolf's reception over the past seventy-five years (a history that includes the propensity to conflate Woolf with her characters) illustrates the power and potential of the collective process of reflecting, contesting, and remaking.[8]

I will touch on Woolf's reception history briefly in my final chapter. Here, following the insights opened up by Smith's *Contingencies of Value*, I offer a few hypotheses that guide my thinking throughout this book. First, creative works that incite the process of reflection, contestation, and remaking are immensely valuable for the cultural self-awareness they inspire. Second, Virginia Woolf's work provides particularly apt examples of creative writing that stimulates this type of reflection, contestation, and remaking. And third, questions of literary value, like questions of moral value, need not (and, ideally, should not) be relegated to traditionalists, conservatives, or the elite. Progressives, nontraditionalists, and common people have a stake in how values are shaped and disseminated, and thus should exercise a voice (beyond iconoclasm) in the communal deliberations that go into the work of valuing.

My third hypothesis was tested most acutely in my first years of teaching at a state university with a student demographic drawn largely from working poor families in East and Central Los Angeles. I was teaching a graduate seminar on literary and cultural theory, which was populated by a dozen high school teachers working toward their MA degree in order to meet the standards for a raise within the Los Angeles Unified School District, and another half-dozen students who held jobs in other areas and who indicated that they were enrolled in the course in order to cultivate their self-professed appreciation for literature. We read two theories of culture that elicited strong responses from both sets of students: John Guillory's *Cultural Capital* and Raymond Williams's "Culture is Ordinary."

Guillory argues that literature has served as a marker of "cultural capital" disseminated by institutions (schools) that reproduce and perpetuate unequal class relations. For Guillory,

> canon formation is best understood as a problem in the constitution and distribution of cultural capital, or more specifically, a problem of access to the means of literary production and consumption. The "means" in question are provided by the school, which regulates and thus distributes cultural capital unequally. The largest context for analyzing the school as an institution is therefore the reproduction of the social order, with all of its various inequities.[9]

This argument resonated strongly with many of my high-school-teaching students, who were routinely exhausted and frequently frustrated by the unequal, inadequately funded, sometimes outright corrupt working conditions in which they labored to teach those for whom the reproduction of class often meant the perpetuation of poverty and inequality. Although good students, many were nevertheless mistrustful of the university, which, while no Harvard or Princeton, still credentialed and thereby served as gatekeeper of what counted as mastery of knowledge about literature and language. That mistrust extended to the less tangible institution I represented – the institution of literary studies – which was widely suspected by these front-line teachers to be the refuge of privileged dilettantes with little knowledge of life on the outskirts of power.

Meanwhile, the half dozen other students in the class (many of whom hailed from the same neighborhoods where my high-school-teaching students worked) gravitated strongly toward Williams's defense of culture as a common birthright. They found in literature a means of expanding their horizons and enriching their experiences of the world. This group felt validated by Williams's viewpoint that "culture is ordinary," shaped and reshaped by ordinary individuals, like themselves, who possess deep, situated knowledge deriving from their place of origin and from their relations with others in that place:

> Every human society has its own shape, its own purposes, its own meanings. Every human society expresses these in institutions, and in arts and learning. The making of a society is the finding of common meanings and directions, and its growth is an active debate and amendment under the pressures of experience, contact, and discovery, writing themselves into the land. The growing society is there, yet it is also made and remade in every individual mind.[10]

For these students – who were not unaware of the cultural imperialism and unequal distribution of cultural capital that my more skeptical high-school-teaching students deftly critiqued – literature provided the opportunity to study the contours of "ordinary common meanings" and to engage in what Williams calls "the special processes of discovery and creative effort."[11] Literature was not, for these students, a dead product of an alien culture to be valorized and then regurgitated on tests (formal and informal) that would open doors for a select few. It represented, instead, a means of expanding one's thought, of participating in the "active debate and amendment" endemic to any cultural formation, whether in the hills of East LA or Williams's Welsh pastureland.

As a young instructor, I was struck forcefully by the realization that both assessments of the value of literature – that of the jaded skeptics and that of the enthusiastic aficionados – were simultaneously valid. This paradox creates the ideal conditions for incubating a debilitating form of cognitive dissonance that plagues many teachers of literature. Fortunately for me, soon after the Williams-versus-Guillory debate, I received the antidote to that particular malady through an encounter with an undergraduate student in my sophomore-level writing and literature course. The student – I'll call her Maria – walked into my cramped, shared office on the tenth floor of one of the high-rise buildings on our campus. She wanted to talk about the first assignment for the class, an analysis of one of Grimm's fairy tales. I admit that I was already somewhat exasperated: I had too little time and too many assignments to grade before my next class to chat (idly, I thought) about the meaning of the red shoes, or the blue beard, weeks before the assignment was due. I asked Maria to open her book (Schilb and Clifford's 1600-page anthology, *Making Literature Matter*) to the tale in question. When it was clear that she did not have the text with her, my exasperation erupted into a self-important mini-lecture on the importance of being prepared for office hours. "I'm sorry I don't have my book," said Maria. "There's a bus strike and I had to ride my bike here. I'll bring it next time." For those who are not familiar with Los Angeles, the prospect of riding a bus any distance through the city, which is not known for its public transportation system, is already daunting. To ride a bicycle several miles through the traffic-jammed streets of central Los Angeles in order to talk with a professor about writing and literature was a form of active resistance to the social, economic, and institutional forces that make "claiming an education" (to quote Adrienne Rich) an act of determined will.[12]

I shut up. I sat down. I opened my own book and placed it in Maria's hands. We turned to the tale and got down to the business of discussing the story and, true to the book's title, making literature matter. To this day, whenever I feel cynical about the importance of literature or the value of teaching it, I remind myself of the hubris that prompted my initial reaction to Maria. Cynicism is a double-edged weapon: it can help to combat complacency about the value of any work, especially work associated with elite culture, but that cynicism can also abet rationalizing narratives about why access to the arts and humanities is (supposedly) not necessary for those who hail from nonelite classes and cultures.

Virginia Woolf herself expressed ambivalence about the complicity of "traditional" or "high" culture in systems of dominance and power in her works – notably (but not exclusively) in *Three Guineas*, where, in a hypothetical address to the honorary treasurer of a women's college fund, she wonders publicly whether she ought to send a guinea to "rebuild the college on the old lines," or to build a new, "adventurous" and idealistic college – or use the guinea to "buy rags and petrol and Bryant & Mays matches and burn the college to the ground?"[13] The fantasy of burning down all the old edifices of higher education and starting from scratch receives serious play in Woolf's hypothetical address, but ultimately she favors pragmatism over destruction because she considers material self-sufficiency necessary (but not sufficient) for "intellectual liberty" or "freedom from unreal loyalties" (TG 36, 78). This freedom, or "disinterestedness," was for her key to cultivating the habits of critical thinking that would allow one to counter the negative impact of "memory and tradition," whether in the form of cultural imperialism or the dominant educational system's reproduction of class and gender relations (TG 18). But material self-sufficiency, for those who were not born into money, depends on employment, which in most cases depends on adequate education. Graduates of her hypothetical women's college would need to obtain employment in order to earn the modicum of financial self-sufficiency that would free them from dependence on patriarchal forces (in the form of financial dependence on fathers and husbands or brothers). Hence, intellectual freedom depends on material circumstances derived from involvement in institutions that tend to compromise intellectual freedom. This is a persistent circle for Woolf (perhaps why *Three Guineas* is peppered with variations on the refrain "here we go round the mulberry tree"), but not necessarily a vicious one (TG 72). Despite her ambivalence about the reproduction of problematic ideologies through cultural production, Woolf maintains a belief in literature's capacity to humanize us, to make us less power-hungry and more capable of rational coexistence and conviviality.[14]

For Woolf, the tension between cynicism and belief sparks a generative paradox that cycles like an *ouroboros*, a snake perpetually eating its own tail: dominant culture influences literary and artistic culture, which in turn tends to reinforce dominant cultural values – but literary and artistic creations also nurture the capacity to think and create for oneself, a capacity that can be employed by those hailing from nondominant cultures to shift or change the cultural values of the dominant. This paradox produces much of the ambivalence that resonates throughout *Three Guineas*, which ultimately asks its implicit audience, the "daughters of educated men," to ante in to the system ambivalently – that is, to gain just enough access to the cycle of cultural production to influence it for the better while maintaining the critical distance of an "outsider" (TG 6; 126).

Noticing, if not naming, Woolf's generative paradox, Cuddy-Keane calls Woolf a "democratic highbrow," unpacking the etymology of the term "highbrow" (and its corollaries "lowbrow" and "middlebrow") and disarticulating it from earlier concepts of the "elite" and the "masses." Citing Williams extensively in her exegesis, Cuddy-Keane argues that intellectual endeavors need not be relegated to the elite classes if "we open ourselves up to new configurations" of culture, where "high" culture is not associated exclusively with elite classes, and the activities and preferences of the working classes not automatically associated with "low" or "mass" culture. These "new configurations" could be made more viable with greater access to education for the entire population and not just the wealthy elites. Thus, Cuddy-Keane asks,

> Are intellectual readers necessarily elite readers if the required knowledge and skills can be made available to all? Is there any reason why intellectual reading cannot be popular, in the sense of arising from a grass-roots, common readers' need? Why should reading for entertainment and relaxation – the

currently prevailing sense of popular – not be seen as complementary to reading for mental stimulation, allowing diverse kinds of reading practice peacefully to coexist?[15]

The debate between the "brows" that Cuddy-Keane examines so aptly has morphed in the twenty-first century, but it is far from obsolete. For Woolf's contemporary, Q. D. Leavis, print journalism (in the form of newspapers and magazines) was the bane of the reading public. When that public did read books, they tended to read what we today call "genre fiction." In her 1939 study, Leavis noted that public libraries (for her a barometer of the reading habits of the "lowbrow" majority) seldom stocked

what is considered by the critical minority to be the significant work in fiction – the novels of D. H. Lawrence, Virginia Woolf, James Joyce, T. F. Powys, and E. M. Forster. Apart from the fact that three out of the five are held by the majority to be indecent, a fact suggestive in itself, four out of the five would convey very little, if anything, to the merely literate.[16]

Citing the popularity of detective fiction and "thrillers" in both public and subscription libraries, Leavis goes so far as to contend that "the reading habit is now often a form of the drug habit."[17]

Seventy years later, electronic media are similarly regarded, ostensibly enfeebling the intellectual and cognitive capacities of the next generation. A 2009 *Guardian* headline, for example, cautions that "Facebook and Bebo Risk 'Infantilising' the Human Mind."[18] One hears echoes of the news clippings Woolf routinely satirized in the *Guardian* description of "Lady Greenfield, professor of synaptic pharmacology" informing the House of Lords that social media "are devoid of cohesive narrative and long-term significance. As a consequence, the mid-21st century mind might almost be infantilised, characterised by short attention spans, sensationalism, inability to empathise and a shaky sense of identity." Lady Greenfield's forewarning, like Leavis's anxiety over readers' addiction to genre fiction, may yet go the way of Wordsworth's 1800 admonition against "frantic novels, sickly and stupid German tragedies" or Matthew Arnold's lament that "Wragg is in custody," for other evidence suggests that the next generations, despite their gadgets and apps, are reading as many, if not more, books than their predecessors.[19] The Pew Research

Center, for example, has found that "Millennials are quite similar to their elders when it comes to the amount of book reading they do, but young adults are more likely to have read a book in the past 12 months."[20] The media format changes, but the central questions remain constant: What do creatively assembled words do *to* and *for* their readership? What should they do? And how do they best do that?

Woolf herself was a proponent of new media (film, photography, the penny post) and was far less dismissive of "lowbrow" tastes than many of her peers. She wrote for mass print periodicals such as *Good Housekeeping, The New York Herald Tribune, The Atlantic*, and *The New Republic* without compunction. She was concerned about access to education and championed the public library.[21] Her letters suggest that she had more faith in the intellectual ability of her readers than some of her critics did. Her complaint was not with the masses, but rather with the bourgeoisie ("middlebrows") who (in her view) did not evolve new standards of aesthetic value, but clung instead to old standards for the sake of keeping up appearances:

> [W]hen we have earned enough to live on, then we live. When the middlebrows, on the contrary, have earned enough to live on, they go on earning enough to buy – what are the things that middlebrows always buy? Queen Anne furniture (faked, but none the less expensive); first editions of dead writers – always the worst; pictures, or reproductions from pictures, by dead painters; houses in what is called "the Georgian style" – but never anything new, never a picture by a living painter, or a chair by a living carpenter, or books by living writers, for to buy living art requires living taste.[22]

The middlebrow is, if we follow Woolf's logic, both alienated from the labor of cultural production (producing not to make an artistic work, but rather to "make" money) and estranged from the products of cultural labor (purchasing "fakes" and reproductions, rather than real artifacts from living artists). In contrast, Woolf emphasizes the "natural" cultural competence of the lowbrow:

> how can you let the middlebrows teach *you* how to write? – you, who write so beautifully when you write naturally, that I would give both my hands to write as you do – for which reason I never attempt it, but do my best to learn the art of writing as a highbrow should. And again, I press on, brandishing a muffin on the point of a tea spoon, how dare the middlebrows teach *you* how to read – Shakespeare for instance? All you have to do is read him.[23]

Woolf's suggestion that a lowbrow doesn't need professional teaching in order to understand Shakespeare echoes her own advice to female students at Hayes Court School in "How Should One Read a Book?": "The only advice, indeed, that one person can give to another about reading is to take no advice, to follow your own instincts, to use your own reason, to come to your own conclusions."[24]

If I were to follow Woolf's advice to the letter, I would have to end this volume here; instead, endeavoring to follow her example rather than her advice, I lay out the evidence and ask my readers to "come to your own conclusions" about how and why an aesthetically complex and intellectually challenging artist such as Woolf still matters in the age of tweets and apps and Instagrams. To contemplate this question opens up a more fundamental conversation about why and how the life of the mind still matters. This pursuit is no less trivial today than it was seventy-three years ago when Woolf, in her last novel, *Between the Acts* (written between 1938 and 1941, some very dark years in European history), depicted a community coming together to rebuild "Civilization ... in ruins ... by human effort" in the course of an ordinary village pageant.[25] The notion of "civilization" carries with it so much baggage of ethnocentric hubris, colonialist exploitation, cultural elitism, and plain old snobbery that one hesitates to recuperate the term for use in a more expansive sense, to describe the development of *civitas* – responsibility to a community or, more colloquially, civics. Yet Woolf herself did not retreat from grappling with value-laden concepts in insightful and often unexpected ways, refashioning the "master's tools" (to paraphrase Audre Lorde) in the service of "mak[ing] happiness" – what the ancient Greeks called *eudemonia* – rather than making conquest over others.[26] Describing the moment of frozen dread one feels when bombers are directly overhead during an air raid, Woolf contends that:

> Directly that fear passes, the mind reaches out and instinctively revives itself by trying to create. Since the room is dark it can create only from memory. It reaches out to the memory of other Augusts – in Bayreuth, listening to Wagner; in Rome, walking over the Campagna; in London. Friends' voices come back. Scraps of poetry return. Each of those thoughts, even in memory, was far more positive, reviving, healing and creative than the dull dread made of fear and hate. Therefore if we are to compensate the young man

for the loss of his glory and of his gun, we must give him access to the creative feelings. We must make happiness. We must free him from the machine. We must bring him out of his prison into the open air.[27]

"Creative feelings," in this scenario, are civilizing, connective ("friends' voices come back"), restorative, and liberating. "Open air" is a persistent motif in Woolf's work, signifying liberation from the constraints of parochial thinking, acquisitive materialism, and moribund allegiance to tradition for tradition's sake. For Woolf, the poet or artist teases open (and in some cases cracks open) the fissures in the hard shell of *habitus* (what we might call normativity or ideology) that deadens our perceptions and makes us susceptible to lockstep thinking. Given the perilous consequences of lockstep thinking – the dehumanization of others; the uncritical valorization of conquest, sacrifice, and violence; the insatiable desire to convert others to one's preferred way of life; the premium on acquisitive rather than communal good – it is not too hyperbolic to suggest that creative thinking is essential to the survival of human civilization, if we imagine civilization as the cultivation of the conditions necessary for human flourishing, for happiness in its nonutilitarian guise. Woolf's work, when read as a whole, shows us why and how the generative life of the mind matters. The task of this book, then, is to trace, through her fiction and critical prose, how Woolf proffers this challenge and lays bare this responsibility for her readers.

This task is not a straightforward one because, as Woolf herself noted in her 1937 BBC broadcast on "Craftsmanship," words are anything but useful; or – to extrapolate from her argument – when we insist on the bare utility of words, we strip them of their power. The power of words lies in their complexity, their polyvalence, and their simultaneous historicity and mutability.[28] To pin down the value of Woolf's words – suggesting, for example, that complex fiction such as Woolf's stimulates neurological responses that enhance our capacity for pattern recognition, empathy, or invention – would be to reduce the power of fiction (Woolf's chosen craft with words) to a utility that belies the more complex and less easily described effects that literature (or the arts and humanities in general) has on a reader or a culture of readers. Words are powerful, Woolf argues in "Craftsmanship," because they refuse to be pinned down, but rather insist on their contextuality and historicity. "In short," Woolf explains, "they hate anything that stamps them with one meaning or confines them to one attitude, for it is their nature to change."[29] Woolf's fiction is similarly averse to being "stamp[ed] with one meaning or confine[d] to one attitude" because its complexity is a hallmark of its artistic virtuosity and its continuing appeal to readers, whose contexts may have evolved and whose attitudes may have changed over the decades since Woolf first wrote and published. To say that the endurance of Woolf's work is due in part to its complexity is perhaps not surprising to those with a scientific inclination, given that complexity often allows for the possibility of evolutionary adaptation (to use a biological analogy) or that creative phase changes take place at the "edge of chaos" (to use a complexity theory or physics analogy). But such a claim would miss an important, arguably immeasurable intangible that complements the complexity of Woolf's work: its beauty. The only way to honestly describe or appreciate the beauty of Woolf's work – or any work of art, if we take Woolf's literary and cultural criticism seriously – is to experience it, in this case through reading and discussing it.

I cannot hope here to reproduce the experience of reading Woolf or discussing her work among peers and companions. Instead, by attending to moments in Woolf's creative and critical writing that themselves elucidate the process of illumination that powerful art engenders, I hope to provoke readers "to follow [their] own instincts, to use [their] own reason, to come to [their] own conclusions" about the value of her work. To do this I read Woolf from the inside out, focusing on four key concepts that Woolf herself identifies in her critical prose and develops in her fiction: happiness (or eudemonia), incandescence, interdependence, and civilization. My impetus for this method is to honor Woolf's own idiosyncratic and intensely provocative critical vocabulary, as well as to revalue the deep attentive reading practices of New Critical close reading without presuming that such a reading would be ahistorical or culturally conservative. Fiction, as Woolf noted in *A Room of One's Own*, is "like a spider's web, attached ever so lightly perhaps, but still attached to life at all four corners"[30] There is an abundance of excellent contextual work on those points of attachment for Woolf – her feminism, her familial situation and experiences of trauma and abuse, her socialism and pacifism, her connections to Bloomsbury, her critique of patriarchal marriage and traditional education, her passionate and sensual love for women, her mental illness, her work as a publisher and literary critic, and so on.[31] Therefore, in this work I focus more intensely on the spider's web of Woolf's own creative work without forgetting that those attachments are there and are well documented by Woolf scholars. Woolf herself was a voracious reader and an advocate of omnivorous and attentive reading, so a self-sustained focus on reading her work from the inside out is consistent with her own deeply generative practice.

To experience that generativity, one must read her work without asking for it to conform to our critical desires, but rather be open to the openness (even vulnerability) that it asks of us as readers. If we approach Woolf's work with this openness, then, like all powerful art, it has the capacity to change us – not because of what it says or means, but because of the habits of mind that it cultivates as we experience it. While it is no doubt possible to approach any work of literature with such openness, the "value" of Woolf's oeuvre is especially enduring because of how compellingly she invites her readers to enter into that experience of openness and transformation.

# 1 Eudemonia: The Necessary Art of Living

For readers who are familiar with the recent scholarly turn to affect studies, or for those who know of Woolf mainly from depictions of her in popular culture (as the brooding and suicidal "Mrs. Woolf" of *The Hours*, for example), the suggestion that "happiness" is a core value for her as a writer and thinker may seem counterintuitive.[1] It is highly likely that Woolf suffered from some form of bipolar disorder that contributed to a number of psychological breakdowns, and her youth especially was inundated by personal losses and traumas, notably the deaths of her mother, half-sister, father, and brother when Woolf was between the ages of thirteen and twenty-four, and her molestation by two older half-brothers, Gerald and George Duckworth.[2] Given that difficult start to her life, and the well-known ending (her 1941 suicide by drowning in the River Ouse), wouldn't one be more likely to associate Woolf with *un*happiness than happiness? Kirsty Martin challenges this notion in a thoughtful essay that situates Woolf's many depictions of fleeting, almost impressionistic happiness within the context of public efforts to bolster "mental well-being" in the U.K. population.[3] Martin's reading, an important corrective to the image of Woolf as a perpetually brooding depressive, considers "happiness" in its vernacular sense – a contented feeling or joyful affect. In what follows, I examine Woolf's imperative to "make happiness" a performative (something one *does*, rather than something one *is*) and Aristotelian "end," something that "is always desirable in itself and never for the sake of something else."[4] For the sake of clarity, I use the term eudemonia (often translated as "happiness") to describe the activity or flourishing that Woolf advocates and cultivates in her work. The less familiar Greek term has the advantage of distinguishing happiness (as affect) from flourishing (as performative process).

This is an important distinction, for, as Sara Ahmed has argued, the concept of "happiness" as affect has been deployed in a way that pathologizes cultural outsiders – "unhappy queers," "feminist kill-joys," or "melancholic migrants" – who may have good reason to express unhappiness with social systems that oppress or marginalize them.[5] The ideology of happiness (as affect), in Ahmed's analysis, suppresses social criticism that might lead to improvements in the conditions for the flourishing of members of oppressed groups. To put it another way, happiness, as coercive affect, can impede eudemonia, a way of living and thriving.

## MOTION OF THE SOUL TOWARD VIRTUOSITY

Woolf read Aristotle's *Poetics* in the Greek in 1905 and, according to philosopher Patricia Curd, would have at the very least been familiar with the *Nicomachean Ethics* through her reading of G. E. Moore's *Principia Ethica*.[6] (The Woolfs owned three copies of the *Nicomachean Ethics*, but I have yet to find indisputable proof that Woolf read the work).[7] Moreover, Woolf was a serious, if "amateur," scholar of Greek as a young woman, an avocation that Theodore Koulouris analyzes carefully in his 2011 book, *Hellenism and Loss in the work of Virginia Woolf.*[8] While I would not go so far as to suggest, as Curd does, that the moral virtues of Woolf's characters (such as Clarissa Dalloway) correspond neatly with Aristotle's ethics, it is clear that the concept of happiness, as eudemonia (something one lived as a continual practice, not merely as emotion or affect), was available to Woolf when she wrote her novels and essays.

Eudemonia is defined by Aristotle as "an activity of soul in accordance with perfect virtue."[9] "Virtue" is W. D. Ross's translation of the Greek aretē, which can also be translated "excellence." We might also think of aretē as "virtuosity," which has less of a moral and more of an artistic connotation, and which is in keeping with Woolf's linking of "honourable activities," "creative feelings," and "making happiness" in "Thoughts on Peace in an Air Raid."[10] Aristotle scholars make a distinction between moral virtue (aretē) and eudemonia, although, according to Richard Parry, the concepts are linked. He explains, "While happiness itself is excellent or virtuous activity of the soul, moral virtue is a disposition to achieve the mean between two extremes in feeling and in action. The missing link is that achieving the mean is also excellent activity of the soul."[11] "Achieving the mean" as an "activity of the soul" is not the same as acting in moderation (repressing one's desires, for example), but, rather, fitting one's action impeccably to one's circumstance – a practice that takes habituation and judgment. Woolf describes this type of "activity of the soul" in "How Should One Read a Book?" when she stresses the importance of freedom and control in making aesthetic judgments:

> To admit authorities, however heavily furred and gowned, into our libraries and let them tell us how to read, what to read, what value to place upon what we read, is to destroy the spirit of freedom which is the breath of those sanctuaries. Everywhere else we may be bound by laws and conventions – there we have none.
>
> But to enjoy freedom, if the platitude is pardonable, we have of course to control ourselves. We must not squander our powers, helplessly and ignorantly, squirting half the house in order to water a single rose-bush; we must train them, exactly and powerfully, here on the very spot.[12]

Woolf's insistence that we "must train" our "powers" of reading, of evaluating, as an exercise of freedom evokes a special form of self-discipline that the ancient Greeks called *askesis* – the practice of self-cultivation that includes both pruning and nurturing. The rose bush needs water if it is to flourish, but it has to be the right amount of water – too much is as damaging as too little – and in the right place at the right time. The image Woolf evokes here is of precision rather than self-denial. On finishing the manuscript of *The Waves*, for example, she writes in her diary, "Yes, it was the greatest stretch of mind I ever knew; certainly the last pages; I don't think they flop as much as usual. And I think I have kept starkly & ascetically to the plan."[13]

Woolf's emphasis on the discipline needed to think and work with precision – determining the "fitness" of a literary form to convey its meaning – is, not coincidentally, a theme in Perry Meisel's comprehensive study of Woolf's apparently unconscious literary and critical indebtedness to Walter Pater. Meisel, too, describes Woolf's practice as askesis, although for Meisel askesis is weighted more toward the pruning aspect of self-discipline and less toward the cultivating (and his transliteration of the Greek, "*ascesis*," highlights its similarity to "ascetic"). Discussing a 1930s diary entry where Woolf meditates on her method of composing *The Waves*, Meisel highlights Woolf's emphasis on "cutting," "clearing," "sharpening," and "making the good phrases shine."[14] For Meisel, "Expressiveness and *ascesis* begin to approach their sought-for identity here, with the ideal of perfect fitness or fusion informing her further ruminations on the novel."[15]

The coincidence of Paterian influence, askesis, and eudemonia is not accidental in Woolf's work. As Meisel notes, Woolf's literary criticism is replete with Paterian language, praising the crystalline, gemlike qualities of prose that flames, glows, is transparent, intense, or incandescent.[16] Woolf derives more than her gem-infused language and a penchant for impersonality from Paterian sensibility, however. She shares with Pater an acute awareness of the fleeting nature of life, its brief temporality and interdependent materiality. Pater conveys what today we would call a posthuman conception of life in the organic imagery of his conclusion to *The Renaissance*:

> Let us begin with that which is without – our physical life. Fix upon it in one of its more exquisite intervals, the moment, for instance, of delicious recoil from the flood of water in summer heat. What is the whole physical life in that moment but a combination of natural elements to which science gives their names? But these elements, phosphorus and lime and delicate fibres, are present not in the human body alone: we detect them in places most remote from it. Our physical life is a perpetual motion of them – the passage of the blood, the wasting and repairing of the lenses of the eye, the modification of the tissues of the brain by every ray of light and sound – processes which science reduces to simpler and more elementary forces. Like the elements of which we are composed, the action of these forces extends beyond us; it rusts iron and ripens corn. Far out on every side of us those elements are broadcast, driven by many forces; and birth and gesture and death and the springing of violets from the grave are but a few out of ten thousand resultant combinations.[17]

If this is what we are – arrangements of cells and molecules and atoms that coalesce into thinking, breathing beings for a time and then disperse into other arrangements of atoms and molecules upon our deaths – and if (as Woolf believed) there is no afterlife to redeem life once it has passed, then how are we to make the best of what Pater calls the "interval" that we are given? The concepts of aretē and eudemonia are integral to the answer Woolf poses through her work, for they align with her atheism and her disdain for both crass materialism and social conformity. Given the late-Victorian denunciations of *fin de siècle* aesthetes such as Pater or Oscar Wilde (who allegedly corrupted the morals of a generation by popularizing art for art's sake), I should note that Woolf's answer is far from amoral. "Making" in general, and "making happiness" in particular, are ethical activities, not merely because they provide alternatives to the activity of destroying in general and destroying populations, habitations, or regions in particular, but also because "making" is a means of building communities, relationships, and habitats.[18]

Rebecca Goldstein notes that the "Ethos of the Extraordinary" (i.e., aretē) provided ancient Greeks a means to contend with the relative insignificance of the human lifespan in the grand march of time. Unlike monotheistic cultures, where the power and beneficence of the deity grant meaning to human life (as a creation of the deity and thus significant for that sake alone), ancient Greek cultures, according to Goldstein, bestowed significance on human life according to the excellence (aretē) with which it was lived. Describing the cultural importance of aretē, Goldstein explains:

> The concern with doing something to rescue yourself from being blotted out by all that vastness of unknowing and uncaring time was felt long before Socrates and Plato arrived to challenge the ethos that had formed itself around it. What can people do to withstand time's drowning out the fact that they once had been? The Ethos of the Extraordinary [aretē] answered that all that a person can do is to enlarge that life by the only means we have, striving to make of it a thing worth the telling, a thing that will have an impact on other minds, so that, being replicated there, it will take on a moreness. Kleos. Live so that others will hear of you. Paltry as it is, it's the only way we have to beat back uncaring time.[19]

One hears echoes of the final lines of *The Waves* – "It is death against whom I ride with my spear couched and my hair flying back like a young man's, like Percival's, when he galloped in India. I strike spurs into my horse. Against you I will fling myself, unvanquished and unyielding, O Death!" – in Goldstein's image of a secular culture attempting "to beat back uncaring time" by making life "a thing worth telling, a thing that will have an impact on other minds."[20]

Woolf lived, thought, and worked during a post-Darwinian era of increased secularization. Her father, Leslie Stephen, resigned his position at Cambridge after a loss of faith and is widely credited for popularizing the term "agnosticism."[21] World War I made the fragility and brevity of life all too clear to Woolf's generation, and accounts of the ignominy and futility of trench warfare undermined earlier confidence – which would have been available to the ancient Greeks – in war as a conduit to aretē, or excellence.

Similarly, the desire to acquire possessions, control lands, or dominate others represented a form of grubby incontinence for Woolf, rather than virtue or excellence. In *A Room of One's Own*, for example, she claims that women,

> speaking generally, will pass a tombstone or a signpost without feeling an irresistible desire to cut their names on it, as Alf, Bert or Chas. must do in obedience to their instinct, which murmurs if it sees a fine woman go by, or even a dog, Ce chien est à moi. And of course it may not be a dog, I thought, remembering Parliament Square, the Sièges Allée and other avenues; it may be a piece of land or a man with curly black hair. (50)

Setting aside for now the question of whether or not women experience or act on such "instinctual" possessive desires (and it is clear to contemporary intersectional scholars of race, postcoloniality, and social class that many women do), Woolf's tone indicates that such activities are more like marking a post to claim one's turf (as the above-referenced dog might do) than they are the movement of a soul in accordance with virtue.

With religion, warfare, imperialism, and crude capitalism proving inadequate to the task of lending significance to the short interval of life, the arts remained one of the few – if not the only – avenues available for making one's life "a thing worth telling." For Woolf, such arts were not confined to the fine arts, but, rather, were "the arts that can be taught cheaply and practiced by poor people; such as medicine, mathematics, music, painting and literature ... the arts of human intercourse; the art of understanding other people's lives and minds, the little arts of talk, of dress, of cookery that are allied with them"

(TG 43). Eudemonia would be an aspiration of participants in the hypothetical experimental college Woolf describes in *Three Guineas*, where they would "explore the ways in which the mind and body can be made to co-operate; discover what new combinations make good wholes in human life" (TG 43).

Woolf hints at the "combinations [that] make good wholes in human life" in her depiction of how life at Oxbridge (her euphemism for the elite colleges Cambridge and Oxford) had grown strained compared to her (admittedly idealized) picture of life at Oxbridge before the advent of the Great War (World War I). Musing after a lavishly catered luncheon at a men's college in Oxbridge, the narrator of *A Room of One's Own* finds the experience "lacking":

> But what was lacking, what was different, I asked myself, listening to the talk? And to answer that question I had to think myself out of the room, back into the past, before the war indeed, and to set before my eyes the model of another luncheon party held in rooms not very far distant from these; but different. Everything was different. Meanwhile the talk went on among the guests, who were many and young, some of this sex, some of that; it went on swimmingly, it went on agreeably, freely, amusingly. And as it went on I set it against the background of that other talk, and as I matched the two together I had no doubt that one was the descendant, the legitimate heir of the other. Nothing was changed; nothing was different save only here I listened with all my ears not entirely to what was being said, but to the murmur or current behind it. Yes, that was it – the change was there. (AROO 11–12)

The change, for Woolf's narrator, has to do with background conditions of sociality. Poetry seems less melodious, less ardent to her since the war. In a fanciful, almost pathetically heteronormative, reverie of Christina Rossetti and Alfred Tennyson singing to each other in late-Victorian verse, the narrator suggests that the beauty has drained out of contemporary poetry, as a symptom of the demystification of relations between the sexes: "When the guns fired in August 1914, did the faces of men and women show so plain in each other's eyes that romance was killed?" she asks. "Certainly it was a shock (to women in particular with their illusions about education, and so on) to see the faces of our rulers in the light of the shell-fire. So ugly they looked – German, English, French – so stupid" (15). The narrator soon corrects herself, perhaps aware of the tipsy sentimentalism of her Tennyson–Rossetti vignette. "But why say 'blame'? Why, if it was an illusion, not praise the catastrophe, whatever it was, that destroyed illusion and put truth in its place?" (15). The "truth," thankfully, is neither so silly as the image of Tennyson and Rossetti singing a duet nor so ugly as the image of blustering politicians leading young men to slaughter in the trenches. It is, however, suffused with temporality and knowledge of life's brevity. Walking away from the lavish luncheon, the narrator, perhaps sobering, becomes aware of this in her surroundings:

> It was the time between the lights when colours undergo their intensification and purples and golds burn in window-panes like the beat of an excitable heart; when for some reason the beauty of the world revealed and yet soon to perish (here I pushed into the garden, for, unwisely, the door was left open and no beadles seemed about), the beauty of the world which is so soon to perish, has two edges, one of laughter, one of anguish, cutting the heart asunder. (16)

## LAUGHTER AND ANGUISH – TWO EDGES, TWO ENDINGS

The capacity to live fully and creatively in the everyday is not a trivial matter for Woolf. It is of profound consequence, for our capacity to seek eudemonia is a marker of our humanity. Our propensity to ignore the importance of well-being (our own and others') leaves us susceptible to modes of living (Pater would call them "habits") that instrumentalize experience. We need not return to Aristotle to contemplate the alienating effects of subsuming human life into a means for others' ends.[22]

Woolf's fiction contains myriad examples of characters who are instrumentalized – or, to put it more plainly, used – by others and thus dehumanized, made into objects or tools for others' ends. Women who are not of the upper classes especially face this predicament in Woolf's novels because the means to live independently are foreclosed to them in a patriarchal culture. The narrator of A Room of One's Own, for example, uncovers evidence of women's status as objects of exchange in sexual relations that can only be called "romantic" from the idealized vantage point of the poet or apologist for the patriarchal status quo:

> Once more I looked up Women, found "position of" and turned to the pages indicated. "Wife-beating", I read, "was a recognized right of man, and was practised without shame by high as well as low ... Similarly," the historian goes on, "the daughter who refused to marry the gentleman of her parents' choice was liable to be locked up, beaten and flung about the room, without any shock being inflicted on public opinion. Marriage was not an affair of personal affection, but of family avarice, particularly in the 'chivalrous' upper classes." ... Indeed, if woman had no existence save in the fiction written by men, one would imagine her a person of the utmost importance; very various; heroic and mean; splendid and sordid; infinitely beautiful and hideous in the extreme; as great as a man, some think even greater. But this is woman in fiction. In fact, as Professor Trevelyan points out, she was locked up, beaten and flung about the room. (AROO 43)

It is no wonder, then, that the romantic "humming" of the heterosexual duet between Rossetti and Tennyson grows tinny in the narrator's ears by the time she reaches Fernham.

Even in the more sympathetic situations that Woolf creates in her fiction, both men and women suffer from the effects of cultural roles that declare women are for *this* (sexual pleasure, reproduction, family maintenance), men are for *that* (money making, war, laying down the law both spiritual and corporeal). In *Jacob's Room*, for example, the character of Florinda is seen through Jacob's eyes as a beautiful body that is perhaps without a mind – "it did occur to Jacob, half-way through dinner, to wonder whether she had a mind."[23] After dinner, Jacob and Florinda retreat to his rooms, where Jacob continues to speculate on her status as a "rational animal" (Aristotle's definition of a human), even as their sexual liaison progresses:

> The problem is insoluble. The body is harnessed to a brain. Beauty goes hand in hand with stupidity. There she sat staring at the fire as she had stared at the broken mustard-pot. In spite of defending indecency, Jacob doubted whether he liked it in the raw. He had a violent reversion towards male society, cloistered rooms, and the works of the classics; and was ready to turn with wrath upon whoever it was who had fashioned life thus. Then Florinda laid her hand upon his knee ... when she looked at him, dumbly, half-guessing, half-understanding, apologizing perhaps, anyhow saying as he had said, "It's none of my fault," straight and beautiful in body, her face like a shell within its cap, then he knew that cloisters and classics are no use whatever. The problem is insoluble. (JR 81–82)

While Florinda is clearly instrumentalized in this transaction ("relationship" would be the wrong word for what goes on between the two), Jacob, too, is stunted by his relegation to segregated male society, despite its comforts, cloisters, and classics. Jacob will ultimately die in World War I. His very masculinity, his membership in male society, makes his body an instrument that can be so used as an expendable object – a chess piece – in a war conducted by others above his station.

Jacob and Florinda are two among the many examples in Woolf's novels of women and men who expend the time of their existence *for* others: Crosby, the Pargiters' servant in *The Years*; Mrs. Ramsay, whose life energy appears to be drained by the needs of the males around her in *To the Lighthouse*; Miss Kilman, who devotes her life (and personality) to the proselytizing mission of her church in *Mrs. Dalloway*; Giles, in *Between the Acts*, who holds an alienating job as a stockbroker in order to keep up appearances at a country home that he can only visit on weekends; and Percival, in *The Waves*, who has no subjectivity of his own, but whose life and death in India (serving the empire) serve as an organizing principle for the subjectivities of the six main characters in the novel.

Rather than elaborate on these examples among many, I turn now to the endings of two of Woolf's novels – *The Voyage Out* and *To the Lighthouse* – for they provide as clear evidence as any of the importance of eudemonia to Woolf's fiction. Thomas Beattie provides a careful reading of Woolf's endings, arguing that:

> While unity, coherence, resolution, and a completed meaning were essential to her satisfaction and to her art, she also perceived that the moments of meaning at the ends of her novels must be placed in the wider context of a vital but unfathomable cosmos, a cosmos that paradoxically frustrates human attempts to achieve certainty yet contains within it our ultimate raison d'être.[24]

Beattie's narratological approach offers an alternative to deconstructive readings of her novels (common in the 1980s, when Beattie published his essay), both affirming her craft and combatting the notion that uncertainty (as *aporia*) leaves one without a reason to exist. Moreover, I argue, the endings of Woolf's novels provide insight into eudemonia as a desirable end and a corrective to the dehumanizing instrumentalization foisted on us by the imperatives of capitalism, militarism, (hetero)sexism, and (implicit or explicit) theocratic dogmatism.

As many scholars have noted, Woolf's first novel, *The Voyage Out*, disrupts the typical bildungsroman formula (which for a female protagonist ends with some version of "Reader, I married him") and thwarts genre expectations for the künstlerroman, since the protagonist, Rachel, dies before she can get married or realize her potential as a musician.[25] The novel concludes, however, not with the end of Rachel but with the continuing-on of another female character, Evelyn Murgatroyd, who escapes the closure of marriage. Evelyn voices a clear and scathing critique of what Herbert Marcuse calls "the ideology of death": the notion that death is more than a biological end, but rather an "essential," "ontological" fact that enables life to be "transcended even though the transcendence may not assume any religious form."[26] This ideology, in contrast to the worldly limits of aretē in the Greek worldview described by Goldstein, makes life itself an instrument of something better to come after, or even as the result of, death. Marcuse explains,

> Man's [sic] empirical existence, his material and contingent life, is then defined in terms of and redeemed by something other than itself: he is said to live in two fundamentally different and even conflicting dimensions, and his "true" existence involves a series of sacrifices in his empirical existence which culminate in the supreme sacrifice – death.[27]

Evelyn refuses the consoling platitudes of her fellow travelers after the death of Rachel, retorting sharply to Mrs. Thornbury's Victorian version of "everything happens for a reason" with "There's no reason – I don't believe there's any reason at all!" (358).[28]

Having thus rejected the ideology of death by refusing to believe that life on earth is lived for a better life after death, Evelyn then rejects the instrumentalizing ideology of marriage, which would enfold a young woman of her class and status into a life lived in service to reproduction of the heteronormative family. Refusing Mr. Perrott's proposal in her last appearance in the novel, Evelyn articulates a commitment to living on rather than settling down into marriage, which to her represents an ending rather than a beginning. "To come to a decision [regarding the proposal] was very difficult to her, because she had a natural dislike of anything final and done with; she liked to go on and on – always on and on" (364). Ultimately she tells Mr. Perrott, "You see, I'm not as simple as most women ... I think I want more," and offers him friendship (366). Calling her a "miracle" that has changed his quiet life into a life of possibility, Mr. Perrott pleads, "Now that I know you, all that has changed. You seem to put such a spirit into everything. Life seems to hold on to so many possibilities that I never dreamt of" (366). To this entreaty, Evelyn responds with the promise of aretē, rather than marriage: "That's splendid! ... Now you'll go back and start all kinds of things and make a great name in the world; and we'll go on being friends whatever happens" (366). From one perspective, Evelyn's response is a mere brush-off – "let's be friends" as a way to let a suitor down easy. If we take Evelyn seriously, though, as genuinely encouraging Mr. Perrott to "go back and start all kinds of things and make a great name in the world," then what she offers is a clear alternative to the foreclosed opportunities represented by either the graveyard or the marriage bed. As she says, she "want[s] more," and Woolf shows her preparing to go off into the world (to Moscow, this time) in an effort to find it.

To the Lighthouse picks up on the story of survivorship that The Voyage Out begins (and that Jacob's Room continues, but through a masculine lens). Like Evelyn, at first a peripheral member of the English clique in Santa Marina who outlives and in some sense continues the story of Rachel after her death, Lily Briscoe is a peripheral, unmarried, and therefore inadequately assimilated, member of the Ramsay's social set who carries on the story of Mrs. Ramsay after her death. Lily's role as a survivor and continuer is much more pronounced in To the Lighthouse, however, suggesting a more deliberate attention to eudemonia and living on in this novel, written over a decade after Woolf's first.

Evelyn exits The Voyage Out with the words, "Left alone, Evelyn walked up and down the path. What did matter then? What was the meaning of it all?" (367). Lily Briscoe takes up these queries midstride in the final section of To the Lighthouse, devoted largely to

Lily's perceptions on returning to the summer house after Mrs. Ramsay's death: "What does it mean then, what can it all mean? Lily Briscoe asked herself, wondering whether, since she had been left alone, it behooved her to go to the kitchen to fetch another cup of coffee or wait here. What does it mean?" (TTL 149). Woolf, through Lily, invites the reader to stay for an answer this time.

If we return to Woolf's imperative to "make happiness" through access to "creative feelings" as an alternative to bloodshed and violence, then it is significant that at the end of *To the Lighthouse*, two artists remain on the shore contemplating the Ramsay's long-deferred voyage to the lighthouse. The poet, Mr. Carmichael, also a peripheral member of the Ramsays' social set, stands as a silent witness to Lily's vigil (waiting for the Ramsays to land) and simultaneous attempt to get her image right, to achieve virtuosity, if only in that moment, with her painting:

> The lawn was the world; they were up here together, on this exalted station, she thought, looking at old Mr Carmichael, who seemed (though they had not said a word all this time) to share her thoughts. And she would never see him again perhaps. He was growing old. Also, she remembered, smiling at the slipper that dangled from his foot, he was growing famous. People said that his poetry was "so beautiful." They went and published things he had written forty years ago. There was a famous man now called Carmichael, she smiled ... Yes, he looked the same, but somebody had said, she recalled, that when he had heard of Andrew Ramsay's death (he was killed in a second by a shell; he should have been a great mathematician) Mr Carmichael had "lost all interest in life." What did it mean – that? she wondered ... She did not know what he had done, when he heard that Andrew was killed, but she felt it in him all the same. (TTL197)

Mr. Carmichael provides a counterpoint to Charles Tansley, the ambitious and brittle young man always seeming to need others (especially women) to shore up his self-esteem. Both men experience deep feelings about the war, but Mr. Carmichael is presented as calm and complete, indifferent to the shifting public opinion of his work, and somehow without rancor even though he has suffered anguish at the loss of a friend. Tansley, on the other hand, has the right intentions, but, in Lily's estimation, the wrong feelings – an imbalance that she associates with his lack of aesthetic appreciation, itself signaling a deficiency of fellow feeling, of compassion:

> She had gone one day into a Hall and heard him speaking during the war. He was denouncing something: he was condemning somebody. He was preaching brotherly love. And all she felt was how could he love his kind who did not know one picture from another, who had stood behind her smoking shag ("fivepence an ounce, Miss Briscoe") and making it his business to tell her women can't write, women can't paint, not so much that he believed it, as that for some odd reason he wished it? (200)

Tansley "upset[s] the proportions of one's world" because his motivations do not match his words or actions (199). While his words pronounce "brotherly love," his comportment communicates contempt or self-righteous superiority. The desire to dominate, to be superior, to exert one's will over others, are all "instincts" that Woolf says lead to war (TG 27, 65, 168). Eudemonia, excellent or virtuous activity of the soul, requires one to temper (as in train) one's words, feelings, ideas, and actions so that they are all in synchrony and thus tending toward the same end: virtuosity, a kind of humane brilliance. The arts, whether the fine arts or the humane arts "of human intercourse; the art of understanding other people's lives and minds, the little arts of talk, of dress, of cookery," help to cultivate those words, feelings, ideas, and actions as well as an understanding of how they interact with each other – the knowledge of "what new combinations make good wholes in human life" (TG 43).

For this reason it is significant that Lily is not alone when she "has her vision" and completes her painting of Mrs. Ramsay. Mr. Carmichael shares something of her feelings, resonates with her, partly because of their shared (although differently situated) histories with the Ramsays, and partly because of a shared sensibility tempered by their creative efforts.

> Then, surging up, puffing slightly, old Mr Carmichael stood beside her, looking like an old pagan god, shaggy, with weeds in his hair and the trident (it was only a French novel) in his hand. He stood by her on the edge of the lawn, swaying a little in his bulk and said, shading his eyes with his hand: "They will have landed," and she felt that she had been right. They had not needed to speak. They had been thinking the same things and he had answered her without her asking him anything. He stood there as if he were spreading his hands over all the weakness and suffering of mankind; she thought he was surveying, tolerantly and compassionately, their final destiny. (211)

This communal affect (for "compassion" derives from the Latin root for "suffering," as in "suffering with") does not bring Mrs. Ramsay or Andrew back, nor assuage the "anguish that cut[s] the heart asunder," but it does keep nihilism and despair at bay without substituting a consoling platitude for the pain of loss, of living on. At this point Lily does gain some literal and figurative perspective on her experiences and is able to arrange them coherently:

> Quickly, as if she were recalled by something over there, she turned to her canvas. There it was – her picture. Yes, with all its greens and blues, its lines running up and across, its attempt at something. It would be hung in the attics, she thought; it would be destroyed. But what did that matter? she asked herself, taking up her brush again. She looked at the steps; they were empty; she looked at her canvas; it was blurred. With a sudden intensity, as if she saw it clear for a second, she drew a line there, in the centre. It was done; it was finished. Yes, she thought, laying down her brush in extreme fatigue, I have had my vision. (211)

Lily's vision does not provide an answer to her original question: "What does it mean then, what can it all mean?" (150). Her activity – which has impelled her toward virtuosity regardless of whether her painting is praised, destroyed, or hung in the attic – has nonetheless provided her a reason to live on, for happiness – eudemonia – turns out to be both an end in itself and a means of connecting her to others who share a disposition to cultivate it.

# 2 Incandescence: Attention and Illumination

Lily Briscoe achieves her "vision" at the end of *To the Lighthouse*, but her vision is not a property of the painting that she sardonically imagines hanging obscurely in some future attic. Rather, the vision that Lily achieves is a habit of mind, a way of seeing the world with what philosopher Iris Murdoch calls "careful and just *attention*."[1] This way of seeing is connected to a concept Woolf introduces in *A Room of One's Own* – "incandescence." She uses the term to describe a "mind" that is "disinterested" – or, at the very least, not self-interested. This is a challenging concept to grapple with, as "disinterestedness" risks being mistaken for "objectivity," implying that one can transcend one's embodied existence and develop a perspective on the world that appears to come from "nowhere" rather than from a living, breathing, human being subject to material, psychological, cultural, and cognitive factors that inform that view. Philosopher Thomas Nagel describes the "view from nowhere" in his theory of the development of objectivity, arguing that objectivity is achieved through transcendence of one's limited perspective.[2] While such transcendence is upheld as an ideal for scientific reasoning, it is ultimately an impossible ideal, for we are embodied, socially situated creatures who can only attempt to reason *as if* we were located "nowhere," rather than coming from somewhere and some*body* in particular. To be clear, incandescence is not this type of "transcendence."

Perry Meisel describes the Paterian resonances of "incandescence," suggesting that Shakespeare, for Woolf, "is the perfect Paterian artist because the implicit flame of his genius has fired out all kinetic residue ... and made his work perfectly expressive of his already luminous temperament."[3] Given that all writers, including

Shakespeare, are situated in particular sociocultural contexts that shape their ways of experiencing the world, they can't help but betray interests, dislikes, or preferences (a preference for Tudors over Plantagenets, for example, or negative perceptions of Jews, Moors, and Frenchmen, or belief in the divine right of kings) in their work. In an interaction akin to the dynamic system that, according to Barbara Herrnstein Smith, determines literary value, a writer's interests and preferences will be seen simply as "truths" or observations about "human nature" if the writer's interests align neatly enough with dominant cultural perspectives. If, on the other hand, a writer's interests are associated with a group (e.g., women, Jews, Moors, or peasants) holding perspectives different from dominant cultural viewpoints, such interests will not be understood as deriving from "human nature," but rather as plaints or grudges that have seeped onto the "neutral" canvas of the work.

Woolf's "epistemic insensitivity" to Shakespeare's more partial perspectives shows that she was not immune to cultural biases, despite her feminist and socialist leanings.[4] These are best acknowledged rather than rationalized away. After all, Woolf admits, "there is a spot the size of a shilling at the back of the head which one can never see for oneself" in the same book in which she declares Shakespeare "incandescent" (AROO 90). Moreover, just before she makes her claim about Shakespeare, she advises her audience of young women at Girton that "What is amusing now ... had to be taken in desperate earnest once. Opinions that one now pastes in a book labelled cock-a-doodle-dum and keeps for reading to select audiences on summer nights once drew tears, I can assure you" (AROO 55–56).

Is it possible to salvage a term such as "incandescence"? Or should we paste it in a book (or blog) to share with select audiences for a laugh? Would terms such as "disinterested" (used by Woolf repeatedly in *Three Guineas*) or "dispassionate" serve better? These terms, too, describe impossible dispositions, despite their less quirky connotations. In her groundbreaking 1988 essay on "situated knowledges," Donna Haraway elucidated the solipsism of supposedly pure objectivity, arguing that there is no position outside of culture from which one can simultaneously partake of culture. To imagine that one could achieve a position of pure disinteredness would involve playing what Haraway calls the "god trick": a fantasy of complete externality to one's self and one's creations.[5] Haraway does not cede ground to theories of outright relativism, however, but instead calls for "epistemologies of location, positioning, and situating, where partiality and not universality is the condition of being heard to make rational knowledge claims ... the view from a body, always a complex, contradictory, structuring and structured body, versus the view from above, from nowhere, from simplicity."[6]

Can there be a *situated incandescence*, then, that would not absolve Woolf (or Shakespeare) of their inability to see the "spot the size of a shilling at the back of the[ir] head[s]," but nevertheless recognize work that clearly moves beyond Hobbesian self-interest?[7] That is, can "incandescence" be thought of not as "objectivity" or lack of investment in an issue, but rather as an attempt to move beyond mere self-interestedness in one's vantage point? Can one develop an epistemology or perspective that is attentive to other's interests as well as one's own? Perhaps the term "incandescence," quirky as it sounds, is more apt than "disinterestedness," for it implies a form of illumination that is heated, rather than cool.[8] The term also calls to mind the incandescent light bulb, invented by British scientist Joseph Swan in 1878.[9] The light bulb is, to be sure, glowing from within, but not without being connected to an infrastructure that has been constructed to supply it with electricity. In a more figurative sense, we can imagine situated incandescence as a source of clarifying illumination that is, nevertheless, connected to human-made networks of power.

At issue for Woolf in this discussion of illumination and connection is what she calls "intellectual liberty," a standpoint achieved through the lessons taught by "poverty, chastity, derision, and freedom from unreal loyalties" (TG 102, 95). I shall discuss Woolf's eccentric recipe for developing intellectual freedom later in this chapter, but I return now to Woolf's original theories of incandescence in *A Room of One's Own* to consider the viability of *situated incandescence* as a critical term.

## EPISTEMIC HUMILITY AND CULTIVATING JUST
## AND LOVING ATTENTION

Just before her praise of Shakespeare, Woolf acknowledges the vanity
of many creative artists:

> Unfortunately, it is precisely the men or women of genius who mind most
> what is said of them. Remember Keats. Remember the words he had cut on
> his tombstone. Think of Tennyson; think – but I need hardly multiply
> instances of the undeniable, if very fortunate, fact that it is the nature of
> the artist to mind excessively what is said about him. Literature is strewn
> with the wreckage of men who have minded beyond reason the opinions of
> others. And this susceptibility of theirs is doubly unfortunate, I thought,
> returning again to my original enquiry into what state of mind is most
> propitious for creative work, because the mind of an artist, in order to
> achieve the prodigious effort of freeing whole and entire the work that is in
> him, must be incandescent, like Shakespeare's mind ... There must be no
> obstacle in it, no foreign matter unconsumed. (AROO 56)

In this context, incandescence looks more like healthy self-esteem
than absolute impartiality. Failed geniuses are apparently too susceptible to peer pressure and public opinion, minding "beyond reason"
what others think of them. Woolf, who lived before the golden age of
self-help books and pop psychology, cannot be making such an argument, can she? No. And, maybe ... yes.

Good writing, for Woolf, should move beyond the self-interest of
the writer, so that the reader can focus on the work itself and not the
ego of the author. Shakespeare is the epitome of the good writer, in her
view, because

> We are not held up by some "revelation" which reminds us of the writer. All
> desire to protest, to preach, to proclaim an injury, to pay off a score, to make
> the world the witness of some hardship or grievance was fired out of him and
> consumed. Therefore his poetry flows from him free and unimpeded. If ever a
> human being got his work expressed completely, it was Shakespeare. If ever a
> mind was incandescent, unimpeded ... it was Shakespeare's mind. (AROO
> 56–57)

If we think of incandescence as the absence (or at least mitigation) of
egotism, rather than as impartiality, then the term offers insight into
what Woolf values in good writing. Woolf's misgivings about egotism
are evident in the distress she displays when confronted, in modern

fiction, with the "dominance of the letter 'I' and the aridity, which, like the beech tree, it casts within its shade" (AROO 100). The self-conscious "I" blocks our view of the world around us, such that the narrow view remaining in its shadow becomes boring (AROO 100). In order to see the world better, one must attempt to "get outside one's own head" in the colloquial and not "god-trick" sense of the phrase. This is where the self-help industry encroaches a bit on Woolf's turf; a quick Google search yields more than 63 million hits for the phrase "get out of one's head." Without digressing too far into the realm of new-age psychology, it is safe to say that "getting out of one's head" entails the habits of "mindfulness," "being present," "cultivating empathy," and "remember[ing] that we have a body attached to our head."[10] So that we don't confuse the colloquial term with the philosophical concept of the "view from nowhere," perhaps I should say that Woolf recommends getting the shadow of the "I" out of one's head.

Directing one's thoughts beyond the shadow of egotism is a practice that has affinity with Iris Murdoch's moral philosophy, particularly as it enables the cultivation of "just attention."[11] Murdoch developed a now well-known thought experiment to explain the concept of just attention, or what she later calls a "just and loving gaze."[12] In Murdoch's vignette, a mother-in-law (M) struggles to overcome her initial perception of her daughter-in-law (D) as "good-hearted" but "unpolished," "tiresomely juvenile," and beneath her son in dignity and status.[13] While always out-wardly behaving impeccably, the mother-in-law nevertheless develops morally, in Murdoch's view:

> Time passes, and it could be that M settles down with a hardened sense of grievance and a fixed picture of D, imprisoned (if I may use a question-begging word) by the cliché: my poor son has married a silly vulgar girl. However, the M of the example is an intelligent and well-intentioned person, capable of self-criticism, capable of giving careful and just *attention* to an object which confronts her. M tells herself: "I am old-fashioned and conven-tional. I may be prejudiced and narrow-minded. I may be snobbish. I am certainly jealous. Let me look again." ... D is discovered to be not vulgar but refreshingly simple, not undignified but spontaneous, not noisy but gay, not tiresomely juvenile but delightfully youthful, and so on. And as I say, ex hypothesi, M's outward behaviour, beautiful from the start, in no way alters.[14]

Such a shift, wholly internal and yet ethically significant (as well as transformative for M), is akin to Lily Brisco's finding her "vision" in the last scene of *To the Lighthouse*, as I shall explain below.[15]

With Murdoch's concept of "just attention" in mind, it is possible to understand "incandescence" as an epistemological shift from an egocentric way of knowing to a contextual way of knowing – not as the evacuation of self or of subjective perspective, but rather as the potential to think from a perspective attuned to others and the world *in relation* to one's self.[16] Incandescence therefore offers the possibility of community formation that attends to the particularities of an individual within the community. This is an important difference from the Paterian notion of experience as "ringed round for each one of us by that thick wall of personality through which no real voice has ever pierced on its way to us," because Woolf acknowledges that we can reach each other through our art, and that connecting with each other is an important ethical imperative.[17] We saw this shift at the end of *To the Lighthouse*, where, as I noted in Chapter 1, Lily and Mr. Carmichael share a sensibility that allows Lily to arrive at a more compassionate view of the Ramsays.[18] Her perspectival shift, which alters none of the material circumstances or plot events in the narrative (being entirely internal to Lily), is yet the denouement of the entire novel.

Situated incandescence also shares affinities with the outsider standpoint that Woolf cultivates in *Three Guineas* as an antidote to the addictive lures of materialism, self-aggrandizement, competition, and the desire to dominate that lead masculine culture inexorably toward war. Endeavoring to maintain women's "intellectual liberty" while encouraging women to enter the professions (rife with the temptations above, which have corrupted men), Woolf turns the tables on dominant privilege and identifies the struggles that women have faced as sources of insight: "If you refuse to be separated from the four great teachers of the daughters of educated men – poverty, chastity, derision and freedom from unreal loyalties – but combine them with some wealth, some knowledge, and some service to real loyalties then you can enter the professions and escape the risks that make them undesirable" (TG 96). These "four great teachers" require some elaboration for their insights into the epistemological shift that Woolf advocates in a theory of situated incandescence. "Poverty," "chastity," "derision," and "freedom from unreal loyalties" are all conditions that the majority of women, in the early twentieth century, would have encountered as a result of oppression in a male-dominated society.

Present-day philosophers have a developed a sophisticated vocabulary for describing the insights that Woolf attributes to "poverty," "chastity," "derision," and "freedom from unreal loyalties." Social epistemologist José Medina, for example, identifies the "epistemic virtues" and "epistemic vices" that arise in unequal social situations, making all parties in a social system – but especially the privileged – less capable knowers:

> In a situation of oppression, epistemic relations are screwed up ... Racist and sexist ideologies make us all cognitively worse off: they instill distrust; they lead people to underestimate or overestimate their cognitive capacities; and they are the breeding ground for all kinds of biases and prejudices that distort perception, judgment, and reasoning. Social injustices typically have a negative impact on our epistemic relations to each other (deteriorating epistemic trust, endangering impartiality, weakening the credibility people ascribe to each other, etc.), and also on our epistemic relations to ourselves (undermining our epistemic confidence, self-trust, and self-reliance; compromising our epistemic goals and projects; weakening our motivation for learning and cognitive improvement, etc.).[19]

Woolf describes these "screwed up" epistemic relations in more vernacular language, but with similar rhetorical force:

> Your class possesses in its own right and not through marriage practically all the capital, all the land, all the valuables, and all the patronage in England. Our class possesses in its own right and not through marriage practically none of the capital, none of the land, none of the valuables, and none of the patronage in England. That such differences make for very considerable differences in mind and body, no psychologist or biologist would deny ... Though we see the same world, we see it through different eyes. (TG 22)

Women and men, in Woolf's example, know the world differently – not because of innate differences, but because of the unequal social relations brought about by sexism and patriarchy.

Medina elaborates on epistemic virtues and epistemic vices that arise in conditions of oppression (and the patriarchal social system

Woolf describes above would count as a "situation of oppression.")
"Epistemic vices," for Medina, arise from the "predicament" of being
situated dominantly in a culture and thus habituated to "a set of
corrupted attitudes and dispositions that get in the way of
knowledge."[20] Importantly, these attitudes are not essential to one's
identity, but rather the result of being socially situated in a particular
position *vis à vis* power. Habituation is key, for one can work to undo
the stultifying effects of one's situatedness (potentially through the
activity of askesis outlined in Chapter 1). Medina counterpoises the
"epistemic vices" of the privileged with the "epistemic virtues" sti-
mulated by conditions of oppression: "On the other hand, an epistemic virtue is a character trait that constitutes an epistemic advantage
for the individual who possesses it and for those who interact with
him or her: roughly, a set of attitudes and dispositions that facilitate
the acquisition and dissemination of knowledge."[21] Epistemic virtues
are not inherent to the person any more than epistemic vices are, but
depend on one's learning from circumstance. Privileged knowers have
less impetus to look at the world in ways that disrupt the status quo,
however, and thus are more susceptible to the vices Medina identifies.
The first of these is "epistemic arrogance."[22] Sounding almost
Woolfian, Medina explains:

> To overestimate one's powers (epistemic or otherwise) can get one in trou-
> ble. Those who grow used to carrying with them the presumption of know-
> ing, of speaking authoritatively, of not being cognitively suspect, have but
> rare opportunities to find out their own limitations. Those who are episte-
> mically spoiled have a hard time learning their mistakes, their biases, and
> the constraints and presuppositions of their position in the world and their
> perspective. Those who are so spoiled are in danger of becoming know-it-alls,
> of thinking themselves cognitively superior. This kind of cognitive self-
> indulgence or cognitive superiority complex is what I will call epistemic
> arrogance.[23]

"Professor von X" in *Room of One's Own* is a prime example of
epistemic arrogance, as are the many experts, bishops, judges, states-
men, and fathers Woolf cites in the numerous and often satirical
footnotes to *Three Guineas*.
   The second epistemic vice Medina associates with the privileged classes is "epistemic laziness" – the "socially produced and

carefully orchestrated lack of curiosity" about the domains of the less privileged.[24] We might think about how much Crosby, the Pargiters' servant in *The Years*, knows about the daily activities and life trajectories of the Pargiter children, and how little they know about her life outside of the moments when it intersects with their own. Or we might call to mind the enormous efforts undertaken by Mrs. McNab and Mrs. Bast, the charwomen who have been asked, with very little consideration of the labor required, to "see that the [Ramsays'] house was ready" for inhabitation after years of neglect (TTL 143).

The third "epistemic vice" identified by Medina is a form of active ignorance rather than passive incuriosity:

> The cognitive predicament of the privileged involves, in some cases, a not needing to know that leads to epistemic laziness, but it also involves, in other cases, a needing not to know that creates blind spots of a different kind: not just areas of epistemic neglect, but areas of an intense but negative cognitive attention, areas of epistemic hiding – experiences, perspectives, or aspects of social life that require an enormous amount of effort to be hidden and ignored.[25]

This form of active ignorance Medina calls "closed-mindedness." Charles Tansley is as good an example as any of closed-mindedness, for his assertions that "Women can't paint, women can't write" are not verified by any evidence but are rather the result of his wish that it be so in order to shore up his own sense of superiority (TTL 51). Woolf includes even more scathing examples of closed-mindedness in her extensive footnotes to *Three Guineas*. In her footnote on the "the symbolic splendor" of masculine dress, for example, she remarks, "The fact that both sexes have a very marked though dissimilar love of dress seems to have escaped the notice of the dominant sex owing largely it must be supposed to the hypnotic power of dominance" (TG 24, 177).

As corollaries to the epistemic vices of the privileged, Medina recognizes three corresponding "epistemic virtues" – "epistemic humility, curiosity/diligence, and open-mindedness."[26] These virtues align remarkably well with the "great teachers" – "poverty," "chastity," "derision," and "freedom from unreal loyalties." Epistemic humility and curiosity both come about as the by-products of "poverty and chastity," for example. Until 1880, as Woolf notes in *A Room of One's Own*, married women were not legally allowed to keep their own property (including money), so that even a well-off woman would become financially dependent on her husband if she chose to marry (AROO 112). The "Sex Qualification (Removal) Act" was passed only in 1919, meaning that generations of women were not able to earn money in the white-collar sphere, although plenty of women from the working classes labored in "menial" positions such as in service (cleaning, cooking, child-rearing for the gentry) or in sweatshops. These conditions led to what Woolf called the great teacher of "poverty," which might predispose women to maintain a balanced perspective on making money:

> These [excerpts from the lives of professional men] make us of the opinion that if people are highly successful in their professions they lose their senses. Sight goes. They have no time to look at pictures. Sound goes. They have no time to listen to music. Speech goes. They have no time for conversation. They lose their sense of proportion – the relations between one thing and another. Humanity goes. Money making becomes so important that they must work by night as well as by day. Health goes. And so competitive do they become that they will not share their work with others though they have more than they can do themselves. What then remains of the human being who has lost sight, and sound, and sense of proportion? (TG 88)

These money-addicted successful men have forgotten a key insight of the "poverty" Woolf advocates – "if extreme wealth is undesirable and extreme poverty is undesirable, it is arguable that there is some mean between the two which is desirable" (TG 84). Their addiction, moreover, leads to a lack of curiosity about the world around them – its music, art, and conviviality. Such epistemic laziness literally disables them, destroying their physical as well as their cognitive health. Woolf thus clarifies her advice to her hypothetical addressee, an honorary treasurer seeking to aid women in the professions: "By poverty is meant enough money to live upon. That is, you must earn enough to be independent of any other human being and to buy that modicum of health, leisure, knowledge and so on that is needed for the full development of body and mind. But no more. Not a penny more" (TG 97).

"Chastity" and "derision" both involve thinking for oneself and not for the sake of others. Woolf writes that, "By chastity is meant that when you have made enough to live on by your profession you must refuse to sell your brain for the sake of money" (TG 97). One can continue to work, think, write, create, but for the sake of that knowledge, art, or activity in itself; or, one can "give the knowledge acquired professionally to those who need it for nothing" (97). Derision one could take as a form of chastity, but in this case one refuses to sell one's brain for the sake of honor or public regard. Woolf notes that, "By derision – a bad word, but once again the English language is much in need of new words – is meant that you must refuse all methods of advertising merit, and hold that ridicule, obscurity, and censure are preferable, for psychological reasons, than fame and praise" (TG 97). This may seem overly strict on Woolf's part, for what could be wrong with a little fame and praise? Insofar as fame and praise can make the practice of epistemic humility (or of getting clear of the shadow of the "I" in one's head) difficult, however, they are potentially toxic. Medina outlines the benefits of epistemic humility in what we might see as an elaboration of Woolf's "psychological reasons":

> Having a humble and self-questioning attitude towards one's cognitive repertoire can lead to many epistemic achievements and advantages: qualifying one's beliefs and making finer-grained discriminations; identifying one's cognitive gaps and what it would take to fill them; being able to formulate questions and doubts for oneself and others; and so on. Insofar as humility involves epistemic attitudes and habits conducive to the identification of cognitive lacunas, it can facilitate the learning process and one's overall cognitive improvement.[27]

"Freedom from unreal loyalties" is perhaps the most difficult of Woolf's imperatives to implement. For Woolf, this freedom requires attention to one's attachments to markers of privilege: "You must rid yourself of pride of nationality in the first place; also of religious pride, college pride, school pride, family pride, sex pride and those unreal loyalties that spring from them" (TG 97). For "pride" – which can be a virtue if well-directed, and an impediment if lacking or misdirected – we may wish to substitute Medina's "closed-mindedness." Unreal loyalties, such as unthinking patriotism, religious chauvinism, or disciplinary tunnel vision, impede one's vision of others and cloud one's ability to see with "just vision." If one is aiming to uphold peace and justice in a complex world such as Woolf's in 1939 or ours in the twenty-first century, then we need all of our powers of cognition and insight to be working without impediment.

## ORLANDO'S INCANDESCENCE

This brings us back to the dilemma of situated incandescence. Can it be a form of epistemic curiosity and open-mindedness, or is incandescence, as Woolf uses it in *A Room of One's Own*, a form of epistemic arrogance or "unreal loyalty"? If incandescence implies the "freedom to think of things in themselves" then we could say, following Medina, that situated incandescence necessitates the cultivation of epistemic virtues (AROO 39). In order to cultivate epistemic virtues, the privileged would need to retrain the habits of thought that often accompany membership in a privileged class. The oppressed would have the arguably more difficult task of sustaining confidence in the legitimacy of their worldview, despite the frequent dismissal or erasure of that worldview by the epistemically arrogant privileged classes.

Woolf's novel *Orlando* depicts the cultivation of epistemic virtue and the gradual relinquishing of epistemic vice by tracing the trajectory of the protagonist's exceptional career as a poet. Best known for its reputation as the "longest and most charming love letter in literature" between Woolf and the poet-novelist Vita Sackville-West, the novel also receives a great deal of attention for its gender bending (Orlando lives his first two hundred or so years as a man and the next couple of hundred years as a woman), its parody of the biography form, and its satirical portrait of the history of English literature.[28] Less serious attention has been paid to Orlando's role as a poet, with the exception of Kari Lokke, who examines Woolf's theory of incandescence in relation to Woolf's "writing and parodying the Romantic sublime."[29] What if we were to take Orlando's development as a poet seriously, however, with an eye to how Woolf's depictions may instruct as well as delight?[30]

We first encounter Orlando as a poetically self-conscious young Elizabethan nobleman who has been raised in all of the conditions that would foster the vice of epistemic arrogance. Indeed, the reader is first introduced to him as he is in the act of "slicing at the head of a Moor which swung from the rafters" (O 11).[31] Not only is Orlando's sex without doubt, his position as an able-bodied and handsome English aristocrat trained in fighting; conditioned to regard non-Christian, non-European, nonwhite men as his enemy; and the heir of a large estate is made clear to the reader in the first two paragraphs of the narrative. No sooner are Orlando's physical virtues extolled than we see him sit down to write his latest play, "Æthelbert: a Tragedy in Five Acts" (O 13).

> Soon he had covered ten pages and more with poetry. He was fluent, evidently, but he was abstract. Vice, Crime, Misery were the personages of his drama; there were Kings and Queens of impossible territories; horrid plots confounded them; noble sentiments suffused them; there was never a word said as he himself would have said it, but all was turned with a fluency and sweetness which, considering his age – he was not yet seventeen – and that the sixteenth century had still some years of its course to run, were remarkable enough. At last, however, he came to a halt. He was describing, as all young poets are for ever describing, nature, and in order to match the shade of green precisely he looked (and here he showed more audacity than most) at the thing itself, which happened to be a laurel bush growing beneath the window. After that, of course, he could write no more. (O 13–14)

It is significant here that Orlando, who churns out prolific amounts of verbiage about the abstract personages and horrid plots of his drama, becomes blocked the moment he attempts to look "at the thing itself" – a catchphrase, as we have seen, for Woolf's notion of incandescence.

Orlando next takes up the pen after a period of solitude and reading precipitated by the end of his disastrous love affair with a Russian princess, Sasha. The narrator is quick to contrast Orlando's material well-being with his literary duress:

> The wretch takes to writing. And while this is bad enough in a poor man, whose only property is a chair and a table set beneath a leaky roof – for he has not much to lose, after all – the plight of a rich man, who has houses and cattle, maidservants, asses and linen, and yet writes books, is pitiable in the extreme. The flavour of it all goes out of him; he is riddled by hot irons; gnawed by vermin. He would give every penny he has (such is the malignity

of the germ) to write one little book and become famous; yet all the gold in
Peru will not buy him the treasure of a well-turned line. (O 56)

Orlando's "plight" is exacerbated by his wealth, as the extravagance of
his writing paraphernalia is juxtaposed with the presumed mediocrity
of his voluminous literary output:

> [H]e crossed the room, took a silver key from his pocket and unlocked the
> doors of a great inlaid cabinet which stood in the corner. Within were some
> fifty drawers of cedar wood and upon each was a paper neatly written in
> Orlando's hand. He paused, as if hesitating which to open. One was inscribed
> "The Death of Ajax", another "The Birth of Pyramus", another "Iphigenia in
> Aulis", another "The Death of Hippolytus", another "Meleager", another
> "The Return of Odysseus", – in fact there was scarcely a single drawer that
> lacked the name of some mythological personage at a crisis of his career. (O
> 56–57)

At this point the narrator expounds portentously on the great change
that is about to overcome Orlando – not his change of sex, which is a
relatively minor change to his consciousness, although of great significance to his social positioning – but rather his fall from being a
man who read and wrote for himself to being one who cared deeply
about what others thought of him. "From love he had suffered the
tortures of the damned. Now, again, he paused and into the breach
thus made leapt Ambition, the harridan, and Poetry, the witch, and
Desire of Fame, the strumpet; all joined hands and made of his heart
their stomping ground" (O 60). As one might expect, one so moti-
vated by "Ambition" and "Desire of Fame," one who has not hear-
kened to the lessons of "derision," cannot achieve a state of
"incandescence" or indifference in poetry. Orlando's epistemic arrogance – for from his position as a rich nobleman he cannot see how
his ambitions might be viewed by Nick Greene, the relatively poor
poet he patronizes – leads to his poetic disgrace. Greene composes a
Dryden-esque satire of Orlando, complete with passages from one of
Orlando's private manuscripts, "which [Greene] found as he
expected, wordy and bombastic in the extreme" (O 70). Orlando
hence gives up his ambition to be a great poet, and burns "in a great
conflagration fifty-seven poetical works," keeping only his youthful
poem "The Oak Tree" from the fire (O 71).

## A CASE STUDY IN EPISTEMIC HUMILITY?

The remainder of the novel spans several hundred years and includes a stint as an ambassador, a revolution, a mysterious sex change, a sojourn with Gypsies, a marathon court battle over Orlando's right to own her estate as a woman, a bathetic formal courtship, a spell among the wits of the eighteenth century, a Victorian marriage, a legal disinheritance, and, eventually, the publication of *The Oak Tree* in the late nineteenth century. Most of these experiences can be seen as an education in epistemic humility for Orlando, whose loss of status due to her sex change has opened her up to derision (if not poverty), whose satirical treatment has cured her of the desire for fame, and whose unreal loyalties have been shattered by her dispossession of titles, home, and rank. Only after she has learned from all of these experiences and has dared to write (defying the whispering spirit of censorious propriety's demand that she make her verse more ladylike) does she complete her poem (O 195). Although the poem does receive critical acclaim, Orlando has written it for the sake of the poetry, seeing the oak tree in itself and bringing its vision to words, rather than for fame:

> What has praise and fame to do with poetry? What has seven editions (the book had already gone into no less) got to do with the value of it? Was not writing poetry a secret transaction, a voice answering a voice? So that all this chatter and praise and blame and meeting people who admired one and meeting people who did not admire one was as ill suited as could be to the thing itself – a voice answering a voice. (O 238)

Given that knowledge is relational, and insofar as there are things one can only know through doing, Orlando's sex change is not incidental to her askesis as a poet. Situated incandescence would take into consideration the epistemic insights that embodiment (especially nondominant embodiment) make available to the knower through everyday practices (habitus). Orlando's sex change, if we read the novel as a chronicle of a writer's development from self-interest to disinterestedness, serves as an epistemic readjustment – that is, her embodiment as a woman has helped her to cultivate the epistemic virtues that her previous embodiment as a man hindered.

Her dispossession and diminished social mobility have offered her insight into the networks of power that surround her, and that insight has burned away the impediments of self-interestedness that clouded Orlando's earlier attempts at poetry.

Reading *Orlando* as a journey toward situated incandescence in the development of a writer aligns it with the theoretical project and preoccupation of *A Room of One's Own*, insofar as it illustrates the relationship between social constraints, material conditions, and what Woolf called getting one's "genius expressed whole and entire" (AROO 72). At first glance, this is a paradoxical alignment, given that the very idea of genius calls to mind the "epistemic arrogance" that Medina exposes as a vice. In part, this paradox depends on which definition of "genius" Woolf had in mind when she penned *A Room*. The colloquial meaning of "genius," which would have been available to Woolf in 1928, connotes a person of superior intellect, someone with extraordinary brainpower. A longer-standing definition of "genius" refers not to a person, but to attributes of a person. The OED defines genius in this sense as "Natural ability or capacity; quality of mind; the special endowments which fit a man [*sic*] for his peculiar work."[32] If we think of genius in this second sense, then Woolf's off-putting comments about Charlotte Brontë in *A Room of One's Own* – "one sees that she will never get her genius expressed whole and entire"– appear more charitable than they initially seem (AROO 72). "She will write in a rage where she should write calmly. She will write foolishly where she should write wisely. She will write of herself where she should write of her characters," Woolf notes, intimating that Brontë's *Jane Eyre* is a "good" novel which is nevertheless stunted by Brontë's lack of "experience," (social) "intercourse," and "travel" (AROO 73).

Whether or not we agree with Woolf's aesthetic valuation of *Jane Eyre*, Woolf's point is not that *Jane Eyre* is damaged because it expresses rage or foolishness, but that for Woolf the rage or foolishness are out of balance – imprecise, if we think of the language of cultivation that accompanies askesis. That emotion is out of balance because Brontë's writing is, according to Woolf, impeded by self-interestedness – "She will write of herself where she should write of her characters"

(AROO 73). Woolf continues her reading of Brontë by speculating on what kind of fiction Brontë might have written had she "somehow possessed more knowledge of the busy world, and towns and regions full of life; more practical experience, and intercourse with her kind and acquaintance with a variety of character" (AROO 73). Woolf intimates here that material conditions influence one's ability to achieve incandescence because incandescence is so imbricated in networks of power, whether they be gendered constraints on mobility, financial constraints based on class or gender, or constraints on social interaction based social mores, prejudices, or insularities. These constraints, if we follow Medina, can be the product of privilege as well as of oppression, insofar as privilege can make one epistemically insensitive (more likely to view the world from the perspective of self-interest) than those who are perpetually forced by their nondominant status to consider the perspectives of dominant culture alongside one's own. The privileged Orlando – the male aristocratic Orlando – is the lesser poet, after all, while the less privileged female Orlando has been schooled by her nondominant positioning and thus can see the oak tree from a perspective that is less self-interested – incandescent, even.

Woolf's peroration at the end of *A Room of One's Own* arrives at a similar destination. First, she notes that the apotheosis of "Shakespeare's sister" – that is, an incandescent female writer – required "preparation" that is material and social. That preparation entails not only material support (£500 and a room of one's own), but also askesis, the development of "the habit of freedom and the courage to write exactly what we think," as well as the capacity to "see human beings not always in their relation to each other but in relation to reality; and the sky too, and the trees or whatever it may be in themselves" (AROO 118). If we imagine seeing things "in themselves" not as a form of pseudo-scientific objectivity, but rather as a form of epistemic humility – resisting egocentric impulses in our practice of looking at the world – then *situated incandescence* can be imagined as a form of radical openness to the world. That openness depends on and fosters our awareness of our interdependence – another key Woolfian insight that I shall explore in the following chapter.

# 3 Interdependence: Pattern and Precarity

Is it possible to cultivate virtuosity (aretē) without succumbing to the kind of arrogance that leads to self-interestedness? Can one strive to be exceptional without falling prey to elitism? These are questions that circle back to the questions of value that Barbara Herrnstein Smith contemplated, for if excellence (aretē) is quality one possesses, then it is something that is *intrinsically* valuable. But if excellence is a practice that involves negotiation – as value does in Smith's theory – then it is social and relational, rather than intrinsic. This relationality is highlighted in another key Woolfian motif: interdependence. Woolf often alludes to social interdependence through the metaphor of the "pattern" or, as in the case of her metaphor for fiction in *A Room of One's Own*, through the image of a web (AROO 41).

For example, in one of the most cited passages from *A Sketch of the Past*, Woolf comments on her capacity for making sense of experience through writing:

> Perhaps this is the strongest pleasure known to me. It is the rapture I get when in writing I seem to be discovering what belongs to what; making a scene come right; making a character come together. From this I reach what I might call a philosophy; at any rate it is a constant idea of mine; that behind the cotton wool is hidden a pattern; that we – I mean all human beings – are connected with this; that the whole world is a work of art; that we are parts of the work of art.[1]

There are many ways to read Woolf's ecstatic insistence on connectedness. Perry Meisel writes of Woolf's repeated imagery of patterns, fabrics, and networks: "These figures or, really, metalanguages, are often organic ones, and suggest a vision of life as a pattern of connections 'drawn out' on 'every leaf on the trees.'"[2] Other critics, among them Julie Kane and Donna Lazenby, interpret the high premium Woolf places on interdependence as a form of mysticism – an emptying of the self and appreciation of our apparent oneness with the world.[3] Yet others, including Gillian Beer, Holly Henry, and Paul Tolliver Brown, show the influence of scientific discourse – Darwinism, astronomy, and quantum physics – on Woolf's conception of the "pattern" behind the "cotton wool" of everyday existence.[4] Beer, for example, argues that "The language of physics chimed with her search for rhythmic prose to give her new working freedoms. She used those freedoms to sound communal experience, even universal experience, and to reveal the lines of force that run through historical moments."[5] Brown contends that "In *To the Lighthouse* ... [Woolf's] concept of space and time remains relative, and she melds Einstein's theories with an additional sense of the permeable boundaries of consciousness between entities that reflects the holistic nature of subatomic phenomena."[6] And Henry notes that Woolf and her contemporary, Olaf Stapledon, "forged literary images of the earth in space as a means of launching a critique of human aggression and war."[7] By giving humans a different perspective, expos- ing our relative minuteness in the immensity of the universe, Henry continues, "advances in astronomy not only served these two moder- nist writers in their articulation of a pacifist politics, but also catalyzed a new sense of the human position in the universe."[8]

These perspectives represent the tip of the iceberg of scholarship on Woolf's deep interest in communalism, on the one hand, and strong attraction to monadism on the other.[9] My aim is not to provide yet another contribution to the already existing work on the overdeter- mined influences (whether spiritual, scientific, or philosophical) that shaped Woolf's understanding of interconnectivity and particularity. Rather, my purpose here in a volume on Woolf's value – communicat- ing the value of reading her work through an exegesis of what the work values – is to explore the insights Woolf opens up to her readers through her sustained and elegant illustrations of the dynamic inter- play between the particular and the structural in her depictions of human interconnection. That is, Woolf invites us to perceive the particle and the wave, the node and the circuitry, the atom and the organism as mutually constitutive components of an interconnected ecology, or "pattern" of living.

Why might it be valuable to be able to perceive particularity (let's call it individuality, since Woolf is primarily interested in persons as particulars) as situated within networked patterns (let's call them ecologies)? If I may be forgiven an evaluative judgment of my own, it is simply more accurate to describe social reality as a complex dynamic system. For example, language, as structuralists and deconstructionists alike have argued, is a massive and complex system within which any one individual's utterance makes sense (if one follows the structuralist line of thinking), or ultimately evades sense (if one follows the deconstructionist path). Or, to choose another example, the intelligibility of identity – a concept that we commonly think of as personal and intrinsic – is dependent on (although not entirely determined by) pre-existing social norms, habits, and beliefs. Recently legible identity categories – such as intersexed, queer, or transsexual – depend on social norms and customs that have, in the past several decades, shifted enough to make such identities intelligible, if not universally respected. The cultural process of shifting legibility is not exclusively a late-twentieth-century phenomenon. It was simply not possible to identify as an American, for example, before the seventeenth century. Nor is it possible today to identify as the King of France, although the category certainly existed in the seventeenth century. Even then, an individual who claimed that identity without social backing would have been in a precarious position vis-á-vis the person whose claim to that identity was upheld by custom and belief.

The interdependence of individuals on social systems for their very identity would seem like a simple and self-evident concept, and yet a strong strain of political and philosophical thought has valued individuation, autonomy, and self-reliance as indispensable virtues. Liberal individualism from Hume to the present provides an example of this strain. Human beings are far from independent monads, however, and Woolf, as a socialist, embraced a worldview that recognized the interdependence of persons, even those who perceive themselves as autonomous. At any moment, we depend on others for sustenance, comfort, information, connection, and belonging. Recognizing that dependence (or, more accurately, interdependence) entails an acknowledgement of our *precarity*, a term that has received critical attention lately (e.g., in Judith Butler's *Precarious Life*), but which has a longer-standing history in public discourse about poverty and economic injustice that can be traced back at least as far as Dorothy Day's 1952 essay, "Poverty and Precarity."[10] We are all, because we are living beings, in a precarious position; we are woundable, killable, and subject to catastrophes (natural and political) beyond our control. Butler draws on this facet of human existence to call for a recognition of our commonality across difference, as woundable, killable beings. From the commonality of "precarious life," she calls for an ethics of recognition and compassion.[11]

This being said, there are limits to our common ground, our human sameness. No social system or ecosystem, no matter how comprehensive or compelling, can without variation determine the individual traits, proclivities, thought patterns, and ultimately iden-tifications of the individuals within the system, despite the preva-lence of myriad dystopian fantasies of posthuman communalism gone awry, from *Brave New World* to the "Borg" of *Star Trek*.[12] There is always some noise in the machine, some quirk, glitch, or resistant patch that makes the replication of identities – no matter how subject to social norms and beliefs – imprecise, messy, and thus apt to mutate over time. This is how social change takes place alongside (indeed, *inside*) of systems that perpetuate continuity.

We can trace Woolf's thinking on our singularity and connect-edness throughout her works. By way of example, I focus here on one of Woolf's most abstract and philosophical texts, *The Waves*, and one of her more concrete and pedagogical texts, *The Years* (which was, after all, originally conceived as a fictional case study to illustrate the theoretical insights of *Three Guineas*). Woolf grasped both the neces-sity of recognizing our dependence on one another and the significance of individuation – the idiosyncratic behaviors, the unruly passions, the defiant iconoclasms which might, over time, precipitate beneficial adaptations in our social ecosystem. Her depictions of particularities and patterns, therefore, are more than fascinating observations – they illuminate the underpinnings of social stasis and the mechanisms of social change.

### INVISIBLE PRESENCES AND IMMENSE FORCES

Describing the process of memoir writing, Woolf muses in her own (posthumously published) memoir:

> Yet it is by such invisible presences [the influence of others] that the "subject of this memoir" is tugged this way and that every day of his life; it is they that keep him in position. Consider what immense forces society brings to play upon each of us, how that society changes from decade to decade; and also from class to class; well, if we cannot analyse these invisible presences, we know very little of the subject of the memoir, and again how futile life-writing becomes. I see myself as a fish in a stream; deflected; held in place; but cannot describe the stream.[13]

Reading this passage as evidence of Woolf's relinquishment of "such analysis, such discriminations" to the "historian," Beer juxtaposes it with Woolf's "picturesque" representations of history in *Between the Acts*, notably in the village pageant depicted near the end of the novel.[14] In such "picture-book" representations, Beer argues, "History is stationary, inhabited by replaceable figures whose individuality is less than their community with other lives lived already, 'with the blue and sailing clouds behind.'"[15]

I read Woolf's fish-in-a-stream passage differently, as a continuation of her meditation on the "pattern" behind the "cotton wool," and, more specifically, her contemplation of a philosophical question that goes back at least to the Oracle at Delphi's injunction to "know thyself": What is the self and its proper relation to the world around it?[16] In this context, individual people are not "replaceable figures" overwhelmed by the static inertia of history, but rather relatively small figures inundated by influences that exceed the self. Attempting to describe the influence of her mother – and, simultaneously, the loss of her mother – on her subsequent life, Woolf therefore spins her theory of "invisible presences" that buffet and waft the seemingly isolated/insulated self:

> Until I was in the forties ... the presence of my mother obsessed me. I could hear her voice, see her, imagine what she would do or say as I went about my day's doings. She was one of the invisible presences who after all play so important a part in every life. This influence, by which I mean the consciousness of other groups impinging upon ourselves; public opinion; what other

people say and think; all those magnets which attract us this way to be like that, or repel us the other and make us different from that; has never been analysed in any of those Lives which I so much enjoy reading, or very superficially.[17]

"The consciousness of other groups," "public opinion," and what contemporary scholars call discourse ("what other people say and think") are thus part of the system (the stream) surrounding the fish of the self.

The stream might also be likened to the background noise of conscious living. Rather than a steady state of awareness, Woolf describes consciousness as "moments of being" that flare up against a backdrop of mere living:

> This leads to a digression, which perhaps may explain a little of my own psychology; even of other people's. Often when I have been writing one of my so-called novels I have been baffled by this same problem; that is, how to describe what I call in my private shorthand – "non-being" ... A great part of every day is not lived consciously. One walks, eats, sees things, deals with what has to be done; the broken vacuum cleaner; ordering dinner; writing orders to Mabel; washing; cooking dinner; bookbinding. When it is a bad day the proportion of non-being is much larger.[18]

Consciousness is not without its peril, for Woolf, however. Her first experiences of "moments of being" come "like a blow from an enemy behind the cotton wool of daily life," but she gradually comes to appreciate such "shocks" through *poesis*, the act of making:

> It is only by putting it into words that I make it whole; this wholeness means that it has lost its power to hurt me; it gives me, perhaps because by doing so I take away the pain, a great delight to put the severed parts together. Perhaps this is the strongest pleasure known to me. It is the rapture I get when in writing I seem to be discovering what belongs to what; making a scene come right; making a character come together.[19]

Poesis, for Woolf, thus entails finding the relation between the part and the whole. Hence, in *A Sketch of the Past*, both of the extended conceits she uses to describe the relation between self and the world – singularity and pattern, fish and stream – depict the oscillation between a particular and a system.

### THE WAVES, COMPLEXITY, AND THE SELF-IN-SYSTEM

This oscillation, or dynamic interplay, between singularity and stasis is a hallmark of what scientists and social scientists call "complex adaptive systems." Describing the field of complexity theory, John Miller and Scott Page suggest that the field's "interest is the in between":

> It is the interest in between stasis and utter chaos. The world tends not to be completely frozen or random, but rather it exists in between these two states … It is the interest in between control and anarchy. We find robust patterns of organization and activity in systems that have no central control or authority … It is the interest in between the continuous and the discrete. The behavior of systems as we transition between the continuous and discrete is often surprising. Many systems do not smoothly move between these two realms, but instead exhibit quite different patterns of behavior, even though from the outside they seem so "close."[20]

Woolf did not have the language of complexity theory available to her, although the "patterns of organization" or "patterns of behavior" Miller and Page describe above would have been ripe for observation, especially in early twentieth-century Europe, when "stasis and utter chaos" or "control and anarchy" were lived experiences of populations enduring revolutions such as the Russian Revolution or Irish Uprising, totalitarian dictatorships such as Nazi Germany or Fascist Italy, and/or the continuity of empires – the Russian or the Austro-Hungarian – unraveling in the span of decades. Moreover, Woolf would have been familiar with the basic theories of Adam Smith, whom Miller and Page consider an early theorist of complexity, through her friendship with John Maynard Keynes.[21]

"The person is evidently immensely complicated," Woolf wrote in her memoir.[22] "Biography is considered complete if it merely accounts for six or seven selves, whereas a person may well have as many thousand," the biographer-narrator of *Orlando* contends (O 226). The world around that person, too, for Woolf, is awash with "invisible presences" and "immense forces." Building on these insights, *The Waves*, arguably Woolf's most poetic text, provides a breathtaking anatomy of the self as complex adaptive system existing and adapting within a yet larger and even more complex adaptive system: the world.

Complex and evolving themselves, each of the six voices of *The Waves* interacts in relation to the other five. All six orbit, as many critics have noted, around the absence of a seventh friend, Percival, who, like Virginia Woolf's mother, dies early in the lives of the protagonists and yet remains an "invisible presence" who shapes and guides the others' thoughts and movements. Kane notes the symmetry between the carbon atom, which James Jeans describes as "six electrons revolving around the appropriate central nucleus, like six planets revolving around a central sun," and the structure of *The Waves*, with its six characters revolving around Percival.[23] Beer reads Percival as "the principle of death as well as of immediate living. He is the seventh, 'Septimus', who converted the six into a magical prime number and who continues to make possible the seven-branched candelabra of friendship after death."[24] These six characters are, for Beer, semi-permeable, with "words and thoughts" that "move freely between people."[25] "In *The Waves*," Beer concludes, "Woolf explores a new form of communality and impersonality."[26]

More than communality and impersonality, I see Woolf exploring the oscillation between precarity and continuity in *The Waves*, an undulation that exposes the self's simultaneous dependency on and isolation from others around it. That is, the self is a singularity caught up in a system, like the ocean waves which break on the shore in the interludes that separate the chapters or strophes of the novel. Each wave is part of the sea and yet recognizable as an individual entity with a particular wavelength, crest height, and trough depth. Only under certain circumstances – tidal forces, wind velocity, distance from the shore – will a wave be formed from water (deep ocean swells being made from energy moving through water molecules), gravitate toward the shore, break, and eddy back into the ocean.[27]

The first glimpse of this interplay between precarity and continuity is in the early childhood section of the novel, after the second interlude, which shows the sun beginning to differentiate shapes from each other: "It sharpened the edges of chairs and tables and stitched white table-cloths with fine gold wires. As the light increased a bud here and there split asunder and shook out flowers, green veined and quivering" (W 19). Also differentiating from each other – becoming clear as individual entities – the six protagonists are sent off to school (one for the girls, one for the boys) in this section. Rhoda, seemingly the most insular and precarious of the six voices, does not find herself reflected to herself as a discrete person:

> "That is my face," said Rhoda, "in the looking-glass behind Susan's shoulder – that face is my face. But I will duck behind her to hide it, for I am not here. I have no face. Other people have faces; Susan and Jinny have faces; they are here. Their world is the real world. The things they lift are heavy. They say Yes, they say No; whereas I shift and change and am seen through in a second." (W 29)

Not only does Rhoda find herself un-mirrored, without a face, but she also lacks the capacity to react to others authentically, relying instead on a conscious effort to mirror others in order to act intelligibly within culture. Her compatriots, Jinny and Susan, "know what to say if spoken to. They laugh really; they get angry really; while I have to look first and do what other people do when they have done it" (W 29). Rhoda is unable to externalize herself enough to navigate the world successfully. Without connectivity, she cannot negotiate the pattern and thus is overwhelmed by her interiority, her particularity.

The drama of precarity and continuity is illustrated further in the next interlude, where the beautiful birds singing "emulously in the clear mourning air" and "lovelily ... descending, delicately declining" begin to grub "down the dark avenues into the unlit world where the leaf rots and the flower has fallen" (W 53). Representing the brutal side of natural continuity alongside the bucolic,

> one of [the birds], beautifully darting accurately alighting, spiked the soft, monstrous body of the defenceless worm, pecked again and yet again, and left it to fester. Down there among the roots where the flowers decayed, gusts of dead smells were wafted; drops formed on the bloated sides of swollen things. The skin of rotten fruit broke, and matter oozed too thick to run. (W 53)

Continuity, at the system level, entails death, decay, and fertilization. In the grand scale of the ecosystem, the loss of individual life is a relatively insignificant step in a larger process. Immediately after this interlude, Bernard, who is on the other side of the continuum from Rhoda regarding his individuation from others, remarks:

> The complexity of things becomes more close ... Every hour something new is unburied in the great bran pie. What am I? I ask. This? No, I am that. Especially now, when I have left a room, and people talking, and the stone flags ring out with my solitary footsteps, and I behold the moon rising, sublimely, indifferently, over the ancient chapel – then it becomes clear that I am not one and simple, but complex and many. Bernard in public, bubbles; in private, is secretive. That is what they do not understand, for they are now undoubtedly discussing me, saying I escape them, am evasive. They do not understand that I have to effect different transitions; have to cover the entrances and exits of several different men who alternately act their parts as Bernard. (W 54)

Unlike Rhoda, who is so withdrawn that she does not have a legible self to show the world, Bernard is too external, too much a part of the pattern, and thus has not the hard edge of self with which to distinguish himself from the world. "The truth is that I need the stimulus of other people. Alone, over my dead fire, I tend to see the thin places in my own stories" Bernard admits (W 57). Recalling his day, he remembers himself as different people depending on the situation: "But now let me ask myself the final question, as I sit over this grey fire, with its naked promontories of black coal, which of these people am I? It depends so much on the room. When I say to myself, 'Bernard,' who comes?" (W 57).

To varying degrees, the other four protagonists oscillate between the particularity of self and the pattern of the world. Louis, for example, is both "clear-cut" and connected to history – something more substantial that he feels through the earth:

> "I have signed my name," said Louis, "already twenty times. I, and again I, and again I. Clear, firm, unequivocal, there it stands, my name. Clear-cut and unequivocal I am too. Yet a vast inheritance of experience is packed in me. I have lived thousands of years. I am like a worm that has eaten its way through the wood of a very old oak beam. But now I am compact; now I am gathered together this fine morning." (W 121)

Susan finds a similar connection to continuity through the earth and its reproductive cycles (human as well as plant). She punctuates her place in the natural cycle much like Louis does his place in the economic cycle of trade and ownership – with "I" and "I" and "I" again:

> I have had peaceful, productive years. I possess all I see. I have grown trees from the seed. I have made ponds in which goldfish hide under broad-leaved lilies. I have netted over strawberry beds and lettuce beds, and stitched the pears and the plums into white bags to keep them safe from the wasps. I have seen my sons and daughters, once netted over like fruit in their cots, break the meshes and walk with me, taller than I am, casting shadows on the grass. (W 138–39)

Neville and Jinny, less grounded by earthy pursuits, are pulled out into the world by eros. Comparing himself to Bernard, Neville asserts, "I am one person – myself. I do not impersonate Catullus, whom I adore. I am the most slavish of students, with here a dictionary; there a notebook in which I enter curious uses of the past participle. But I cannot go on forever cutting these ancient inscriptions clearer with a knife" (W 62).

This sharpness, this absorption in the details of a dead language, almost damns Neville to a life of desiccated pedantry, but he is carried away and compelled to connect with those outside himself by his love for another man. Speaking to Bernard, he comes out of the closet by sharing with him the love poems written for the unnamed beloved (perhaps Percival):

> I am asking you (as I stand with my back to you) to take my life in your hands and tell me whether I am doomed always to cause repulsion in those I love?
>     I stand with my back to you fidgeting. No my hands are now perfectly still. Precisely, opening a space in the bookcase, I insert *Don Juan*; there. I would rather be loved, I would rather be famous than follow perfection through the sand. (W 63)

The exchange between the two men transforms both of them, at least momentarily, for if Neville is called out of himself, Bernard is called in by the interaction with his friend:

> O friendship, how piercing are your darts – there, there, again there. He looked at me, turning to face me; he gave me his poem. All mists curl off the roof of my being. That confidence I shall keep to my dying day. Like a long wave, like a roll of heavy waters, he went over me, his devastating presence – dragging me open, laying bare the pebbles on the shore of my soul. It was humiliating; I was turned to small stones. All semblances were

rolled up. "You are not Byron; you are yourself." To be contracted by another person into a single being – how strange. (W63)

Woolf's figurative language in "like a long wave, like a roll of heavy waters, he went over me" evokes the image of a tidal force. Bernard and Neville can be seen as separate moons or planets orbiting an unnamed center. Neville's outward movement – his gift of his poems, his sharing of his confidences – represents his low tide, with the waves pulling away from him and pouring into Bernard's corresponding high tide. The motion not only "contracts" Bernard, but complements him: if he is diffuse and bubbly when he is out in the world, Neville brings him back to a discreet sense of himself.

Jinny, effervescent and polyamorous, appears at first to be conventionally feminine, defined through her physical attractiveness, perceived simultaneously as a threat and a lure. Mark Hussey suggests that "Jinny ... is at one extreme of the scale of ways in which the body can be lived; she can imagine nothing 'beyond the circle cast by my body' (W 92). Her sense of unity projects itself through her body and affects others, as she is aware."[28] Jinny's embodiment, however, does lead her outward, like Plato's cave dwellers who, after having seen the world by the light of the sun, can no longer be content in a society that sits chained to the wall watching shadows:[29]

> But we who live in the body see with the body's imagination things in outline. I see rocks in bright sunshine. I cannot take these facts into some cave and, shading my eyes, grade their yellows, blues, umbers into one substance. I cannot remain seated for long. I must jump and go. The coach may start from Picadilly. I drop all these facts – diamonds, withered hands, china pots and the rest of it, as a monkey drops nuts from its naked paws. I cannot tell you if life is this or that. I am going to push out into the heterogeneous crowd. I am going to be buffeted; to be flung up, and flung down, among men, like a ship on the sea. (W 128)

Like Neville – who, in the very next monologue, says, "There can be no doubt, I thought, pushing aside the newspaper, that our mean lives, unsightly as they are, put on splendor and have meaning only under the eyes of love" – Jinny's sensual life ennobles her, gets her out of the cave and into the world, and becomes for her a form of aretē. This is a paradoxical version of Plato's "Allegory of the Cave," given that, for Plato, the world of the senses (sight, sound, touch, taste, smell) is less real than the world of the intellect. Jinny's world outside the cave is kinetic and connected, but – if we follow the Platonic allusion to its logical end – no less valuable, and, perhaps, no less wise.[30]

## THE BODY, VULNERABILITY, AND THE "ARMY OF THE UPRIGHT"

Woolf's penultimate novel, *The Years*, is written in a much different register to that of *The Waves*. *The Waves* is poetic and tightly concentric, while *The Years* is narrative and sprawling. *The Waves*, despite Jinny's leap to embodied wisdom, is largely a novel of thought and vision, while *The Years* is a novel of bodies and social interactions. Despite its different register, *The Years* nevertheless takes up the thread of precarity and continuity Woolf spins in *The Waves*, weaving it into a plaid of atypicality and normativity crosshatched with interdependence and autonomy. To trace this weft it will be necessary to shift from metaphysics to social theory – particularly "crip theory," a blend of disability studies and queer theory which analyzes how "biopower" (a networked circuit of forces allowing some people and some bodies more access to the resources necessary to have a livable life and others less access to such resources) operates by extruding norms that make some lives more culturally legible and others monstrous, freakish, or deviant.[31] Judith Butler explains that "The norms that govern idealized human anatomy thus work to produce a differential sense of who is human and who is not, which lives are livable, and which are not."[32]

Musing on the "question of human, of who counts as the human, and the related question of whose lives count as lives," Judith Butler brings queer theory back to the concept of "flourishing":[33]

> What makes for a livable world is no idle question. It is not merely a question for philosophers. It is posed in various idioms all the time by people in various walks of life. If that makes them all philosophers, then that is a conclusion I am happy to embrace. It becomes a question for ethics, I think, not only when we ask the personal question, what makes my own life bearable, but when we ask, from a position of power, and from the point of

view of distributive justice, what makes, or ought to make, the lives of others bearable?[34]

The answer to Butler's question goes beyond recognition or rights and touches on the concept of eudemonia, often translated as happiness (as I noted in Chapter 1). The conditions necessary for eudemonia are the conditions for ensuring a "bearable" life. Material well-being and political freedom are necessary for eudemonia, which is why Butler insists that the question of what makes "the lives of others bearable" be asked from the position of "distributive justice." As I noted in Chapter 2, Woolf recognized that material well-being – "enough money to live on … to buy that modicum of health, leisure, knowledge and so on" – is necessary for flourishing, "for the full development of the body and mind" (TG 97). Articulating what might be seen as an Aristotelian mean, she suggests that we need "enough," but not too much – "not a penny more" (TG 97). Material well-being is necessary for flourishing (i.e., living a "bearable" life), but it is not sufficient.

Woolf does not have a spotless record on the question of "what makes, or ought to make the lives of others bearable." Maren Linett, for example, identifies a persistent strain of ableism in Woolf's feminism, exemplified by instances in *A Room of One's Own* and *The Years*, where women whose lives have been thwarted by patriarchy are described as "twisted," "deformed," "cramped," and "like cripples in a cave."[35]

In a powerful essay asking "If the mentally 'deficient' subject, whose mind is presumed to defy any theory of mind, were taken as both a modernist subject and as a modernist 'object of thought,' what insights might an effort of sympathetic intuition yield about its unique interiority and about compositions of interiority more generally?" Janet Lyon analyzes "an infamous entry in the 1915 journal of Virginia Woolf, which reports a chance encounter with 'a long line of imbeciles' on a towpath near Kingston. 'It was perfectly horrible,' [Woolf] writes. 'They should certainly be killed.'"[36] Hermione Lee, whose biography of Woolf is comprehensive and nuanced, attributes the violence of Woolf's reaction to seeing a group of men with

cognitive disabilities to Woolf's own experiences of institutionaliza-
tion for mental illness in 1915 – "This violent endorsement of an
extreme theory of eugenics, written between two very severe breakdowns, must be understood as expressing her dread and horror of what
she thought of as her own loss of control."[37] Lyon reads the shock of
recognition (Woolf's "dawning" awareness that the men she encounters along the road are wards of an asylum for "imbeciles" [a legal
designation at the time]) as integral to Woolf's modernist aesthetics,
while at the same time providing a glimpse for Woolf of her own sense
of precarity, her affinity with the men she despises. "This kind of
shock, for someone like Woolf, must surely extend to her own tenuous
mental sovereignty," writes Lyon.[38] It is important to hold Woolf's
ableism up for scrutiny, even if it contains elements of internalized
oppression. As Lyon elegantly states:

> One may plan (heroically) to kill Septimus in order to save him from the
> Foucauldian nightmare of the institution, while at the same time wishing
> death upon "defectives" for their insufficient institutionalization. Surely
> Woolf recognizes the violence of this ethical contradiction on some level,
> for the idiot boy remains with her to the end of her life, in both his real,
> tactile form, with hand outstretched, and as an enigma haunting the bestial
> face that she dreams about in the *mise en abyme* of a hall mirror. He is her
> *frère*, her *semblable*.[39]

Woolf's own precarity is part of a pattern in her plaid that runs two
directions – one toward recognition and justice for those excluded or
made monstrous by the norm, and another in the troubling direction
of the norm.

With that said, Woolf does pen what is still one of the most
cogent critiques of biopower in fiction. Linking claims about the
health of the nation to masculine mental health, to heteronormativity, to war and colonialism, she satirizes the Harley Street specialist's
worship of "divine proportion" in *Mrs. Dalloway*:

> Worshipping proportion, Sir William not only prospered himself but made
> England prosper, secluded her lunatics, forbade childbirth, penalised despair,
> made it impossible for the unfit to propagate their views until they, too,
> shared his sense of proportion – his, if they were men, Lady Bradshaw's if
> they were women (she embroidered, knitted, spent four nights out of seven at
> home with her son), so that not only did his colleagues respect him, his
> subordinates fear him, but the friends and relations of his patients felt for

him the keenest gratitude for insisting that these prophetic Christs and Christesses, who prophesied the end of the world, or the advent of God, should drink milk in bed, as Sir William ordered.[40]

Sir William's fanaticism about proportion, although exaggerated, is in keeping with what disability theorist Lennard Davis calls the construction of normalcy in the nineteenth century. Davis argues that the "concept of the norm or average enters European culture, or at least the European Languages, only in the nineteenth century," and that uptake of this concept arises from the development of "that branch of knowledge known as statistics."[41] Practitioners of the new field of statistics such as Adolphe Quetelet and Sir Francis Galton heralded a discursive shift from emulation of the ideal man (gender exclusivity intended) to idealization of the average man. Davis argues that, "In formulating *l'homme moyen*, Quetelet is also providing a justification of *les classes moyenes* [sic]. With bourgeois hegemony comes scientific justification for moderation and middle-class ideology. The average man, the body of the man in the middle, becomes the exemplar of the middle way of life."[42] Davis further points out that the prominent nineteenth-century statisticians were also, not coincidentally, eugenicists. Eugenicists such as Galton reimagined the normal distribution that is part of any bell curve as a kind of hierarchy, with the low tail of the curve considered undesirable degeneracy and the high tail of the curve representing Darwinian progress.

For Davis, this "new ideal of ranked order is powered by the imperative of the norm, and then supplemented by the notion of progress, human perfectibility, and the elimination of deviance to create a dominating hegemonic vision of what the human body should be."[43] The aim of eugenicists – including many Fabians known to Woolf, such as Beatrice and Sidney Webb – was to shift that median point in the direction of the top quartile and to eliminate or dramatically reduce the number of people who exhibited traits that fell into the bottom quartile.[44] For thinkers in a milieu heavily influenced by Darwin, this shift would take place through sexual selection *for* socially "useful" traits like height and strength and intelligence and *against* socially "harmful" traits such as "feeble mindedness" or clubbed feet or dwarfism. Here sexual normativity intersects with able-bodied normativity insofar as proper desire (i.e., sexual desire that would lead to the desired eugenicist shift in the median on the bell curve) is desire for able-bodiedness. Desire for anything else was deemed at best wasteful and at worst degenerative. In Canada and the United States, persons considered to be cognitively disabled (i.e., deemed to be "mental defectives") were often involuntarily sterilized, as well as in more notoriously eugenicist states such as Nazi Germany. This practice apparently went on in Alberta until 1972 and in many U.S. states until the 1960s and 1970s, to cite some of the more egregious examples in North America.[45] Homosexual men were also subjected to voluntary or involuntary castration as a supposed cure for their deviant sexual desire.[46] Alan Turing, a pathbreaking computer scientist and celebrated British cryptographer, was chemically castrated in 1952 following his arrest for homosexual offenses.[47] Woolf, too, was told by her medical doctors that she must not reproduce at a time when "healthy" women of her race and class were being told that it was their primary duty to reproduce.[48] Biopower here works through the bell curve – valorizing the norm and then (re)producing it through violence and/or prohibition.

The habit of "worshipping divine proportion" through the idealization of norms brought into existence not only sexual minority identities – a process Foucault referred to when he suggested that "The nineteenth-century homosexual became a personage, a past, a case history, and a childhood, in addition to being a type of life, a life form" – but also the characterization of disabled people as "personage [s]," "past[s]," "case histor[ies]," "childhood[s]," and "types."[49] These "deviant" types, whether deviating from sexual, physical, cognitive, or behavioral norms, bolster the construction of what Rosmarie Garland Thomson calls the "normate," a figure she analyzes in terms of physical disability, and which crip theorists such as Abby L. Wilkerson have analyzed in relation to sexual and gender norms. The concept of the normate, Garland Thomson explains, is a "neologism [that] names the veiled subject position of cultural self, the figure outlined by the array of deviant others whose marked bodies shore up the normate's boundaries."[50] In *Mrs. Dalloway* the law is literally "on the side of the normal"; it gives Dr. Bradshaw the power to commit Septimus Warren Smith against his will (and against his wife's will) to one of Bradshaw's rest cure "homes" – "It was a question of law."[51]

While *Mrs. Dalloway*, through the figure of Septimus, exposes the violence of the norm spectacularly, *The Years* illustrates how normativity is cultivated through continuity in the story of three generations of the Pargiter family.[52] Very early in the 1880 portion of the narrative, we learn that the paterfamilias, Colonel Abel Pargiter (the pun on "able" may or may not be intended), lost two fingers in "the Mutiny," presumably the 1857 Indian rebellion against the British East India Company, often referred to as the "Sepoy" mutiny. We first learn of Abel's injury in relation to a sexual encounter he has with his mistress – "He drew her to him; he kissed her on the nape of the neck; and then the hand that had lost two fingers began to fumble rather lower down where the neck joins the shoulders" (TY 9) – but more often than not, his disability is associated with his role as the dispenser of money:

> He put his hand into his trouser pocket and brought out a handful of silver. His children watched him as he tried to single out one sixpence from all the florins. He had lost two fingers of the right hand in the Mutiny, and the muscles had shrunk so that the right hand resembled the claw of some aged bird. He shuffled and fumbled; but as he always ignored the injury, his children dared not help him. The shiny knobs of the mutilated fingers fascinated Rose. (TY 13)

While Abel's age, retirement, and wife's illness leave him feeling gloomy and "out of it all" (Mrs. D 5), his physical deformity is no bar to his access to places of privilege, such as his club, or social and economic standing. He is not only the paterfamilias of a large Victorian household at Abercorn Terrace (a "respectable" neighborhood), he is also financially well-off, consoling himself at one point for being "richer" than his "distinguished" brother, Digby (TY 125). In other words, although Abel is not "at the top of his tree," he is a respectable – if predictable and curmudgeonly – bourgeois Victorian man.

Abel's physical deformity, obtained during military duty, is a signifier of his masculine value, unlike Sara's, which, although acquired early when someone dropped her as a baby, somehow expresses her plainness and unsuitability for marriage; or Crosby's "rheumatics," which are a symptom of her relegation to a life of servitude as a lower class person relegated to a life of serving the upper classes (TY 122, 221). Hence, Abel's clawlike fingers seem to be always performing (fumblingly, to be sure) masculine activities – paying for cabs, caressing his mistress, and, in Edward's memory, appreciatively flourishing expensive glasses of port. These activities attest to his success, his mastery in an imperial and capitalist system.

In his history of disability and military culture, David Serlin notes that by the late nineteenth and early twentieth centuries, men were scrutinized and measured for their body type, proper (heteronormative) sexually proclivities, and physical soundness. Based on these biometric screenings they were declared either fit or unfit "types" for military service. The fact that war is probably the most disabling of occupations is an ironic corollary to the insistence that military recruits meet high standards (we might say *the* standards) for able-bodiedness. As Serlin explains, to be disabled during a battle is proof that one once was ideally able:

> Disability acquired on the battlefield, however, was another matter altogether. For many veterans of the Civil War, the amputation stump, the artificial limb, or any other overt physical evidence of injury became shorthand for military service. In certain ways, disability became part of a uniform worn by both participants in and spectators of the brutalities of war. Medical photography, and portrait photography more broadly, helped transform the popular image of soldiering and military culture in general. The material evidence of physical wounds blurred with tacit forms of democratic participation and sacrifice.[53]

Sara, Crosby, and Nicholas, in contrast to the disfigured Abel, are depicted as unfit and extraneous to the generational throughline of the story. Nicholas, who "ought to be in prison" (TY 297) because he is presumably a homosexual, loses his patronym and is known instead as the person they (the respectable English people) call "Brown" (TY 315). The other characters, notably Eleanor and North, demonstrate their liberal "flexibility" (to cite Robert McRuer) through their tolerance for him.[54] He is a catalyst for their character development but not a person in his own right. Similarly, Martin exercises his beneficence through his compassionate, yet patronizing attitude toward Crosby. "I'm Crosby's God," he even remarks, a little disdainfully, to Sara (TY 230). And Sara we first see described through the eyes of Abel:

> She [Eugenie] held out her hand partly to coax the little girl, partly, Abel guessed, in order to conceal the very slight deformity that always made him uncomfortable. She had been dropped when she was a baby; one shoulder was slightly higher than the other; it made him feel squeamish; he could not bear the least deformity in a child. It did not affect her spirits, however. She skipped up to him, whirling round on her toe, and kissed him lightly on the cheek. Then she tugged at her sister's frock, and they both rushed away into the back room laughing. (TY 122)

Unlike Abel, Sara never gains access to the places of privilege and status. She can be her cousin Martin's guest at a "chop house," but she is not invited, as her sister Maggie is, to dine in a shiny ballroom next to a "man in gold lace" (TY 139). Nor does she have the class-based access to a home on the "respectable" side of town, perhaps due to the fact that she does not marry, whether by choice or because she is not deemed "marriageable" because of her physical atypicality.

But Sara's story is in the middle portion of the text, not the conclusion. As a project that offers a genealogy of the "worship of proportion," *The Years* does not end without giving readers a critical opening to imagine other ways to make sense of our differences or deviations from the norm. The third generation of Pargiters, Peggy and North, hint at the possibility of those other ways. In the final, "Present Day," chapter of the novel, North has returned to England after a post–World War I stint as a farmer in Africa. He therefore bears with him the traces of colonialism and militarism, but, unlike Percival from *The Waves*, he is not frozen in that moment. In keeping with the *longue durée* of the novel (as opposed to the tight, diurnal cycle of *The Waves*), North's character is allowed to evolve. His evolution might also be contrasted with Jacob's status in *Jacob's Room* – fixed by death into the eternal youth who believes women are beautiful but brainless. North, on the other hand, demonstrates (a sometimes bemused) respect not just for his aunts and older female cousins, but also for Nicholas, the queer foreigner:

> For instance, this evening at Eleanor's there was a man there with a foreign accent who squeezed lemon into his tea. Who might he be, he wondered? "One of Nell's dentists," said his sister Peggy, wrinkling her lip. For they all had lines cut, phrases ready-made. But that was the silent man on the sofa. It was the other one he meant – squeezing lemon in his tea. "We call him Brown," she murmured. Why Brown if he's a foreigner, he wondered. Anyhow they all romanticized solitude and savagery … except this man Brown, who had said something that interested him. "If we do not know ourselves, how can we know other people?" (TY 309)

With their "ready-made" phrases and their romanticism of North's colonial experience, the guests at Eleanor's tea fall back on normatizing discourse. North, however, breaks the flow of that discourse by giving "just attention" (to return to Iris Murdoch's theory of ethical vision) to Nicholas. He may even, in this moment, be practicing the kind of self-knowledge that Nicholas (paraphrasing Plato) recommends, for he of all the guests appears open to knowing Nicholas.

Later, at another social gathering, North questions Eleanor's "sacrifice," as the eldest daughter, to a life of caring for the paterfamilias after her mother dies: "He looked at her. She had never married. Why not? he wondered. Sacrificed to the family, he supposed – old Grandpapa without any fingers" (TY 372). On the other hand, Peggy, also unmarried, is not regarded as an unfortunate spinster. She has a part in the reproductive throughline of the story, but not in the normative female role of mother. She is a doctor who helps to bring about the next generation by attending births – that is, by facilitating the births of other women's children. This is an alternative means of impacting the future, and one that is perhaps less territorial and possessive than the normative alternative posed by Milly (one of Eleanor Pargiter's sisters) and Gibbs, a friend of the family whom we first meet as an average, but healthy undergraduate, unlike the exceptional, but queer Tony Ashton. In what we might call a critically crip turn, North describes the now married and middle-aged Gibbses as "a parody, a travesty, an excrescence that had overgrown the form within" (TY 379).

Across the room in the hall where the Pargiters are gathered, Peggy muses separately on whether happiness is appropriate (if indeed possible) when war, death, and suffering loom so close to the horizon:

> The far-away sounds, the suggestion they brought in of other worlds, indifferent to this world, of people toiling, grinding, in the heart of darkness, in the depths of night, made her say over Eleanor's words, Happy in this world, happy with happy with living people. But how can one be "happy," she asked herself, in a world bursting with misery? On every placard at every street corner was Death; or worse – tyranny; brutality; torture; the fall of civilization; the end of freedom. We here, she thought, are only sheltering under a leaf, which will be destroyed. (TY 388)

She then is momentarily jolted out of her funk by the sound of her uncle and brother laughing at the portrait of a "monster" that the party guests have drawn in a game where each player depicts a part of a body without looking at the other parts that have been drawn and folded over before passing the drawing to the next player.

> "I drew that – I drew that – I drew that!" said Renny, pointing to the legs from which a long tail of ribbon depended. She laughed, laughed, laughed; she could not help laughing.
>      "The face that launched a thousand ships!" said North, pointing to another part of the monster's person. They all laughed again. She stopped laughing; her lips smoothed themselves out. (TY 389)

It is not clear whether the "monstrosity" of the chimeric drawing or North's allusion to Helen of Troy and therefore war – "the fall of civilization" that has been preoccupying Peggy – causes her to stop laughing. We do know, however, that Peggy is compelled to speak at this moment, and that her halting speech turns into a critique of heteronormativity: "'Look here ...' she began. She wanted to express something that she felt to be very important; about a world in which people were whole, in which people were free ... But they were laughing; she was serious. 'Look here ... ' she began again" (TY 390; ellipses in original). Valuing wholeness, Peggy's speech is far from whole; rather, it is delivered in bits and starts, heavily punctuated by ellipses. Her relatives are, she says, discussing her brother North, "' ... How he's to live, where he's to live,' she went on. ' ... But what's the use, what's the point of saying that?'" (TY 390; ellipses in original). The gist of their conversation lacks meaning, she suggests, because what he will do seems predetermined by the logic of heteronormativity:

> "What's the use?" she said, facing him. "You'll marry. You'll have children. What'll you do then? Make money. Write little books to make money ... "
> She had got it wrong. She had meant to say something impersonal, but she was being personal. It was done now however; she must flounder on now.
> "You'll write one little book, and then another little book," she said viciously, "instead of living ... living differently." (TY 390–91; ellipses in original)

"Little books" and children are ironically juxtaposed here, as one might think that for a writer the production of books would have some value, even if the traditional throughline of heteroreproductivity is deemed pointless.

Peggy's outburst at a party filled with guests, especially given the philosophical question – how to live – embedded near the beginning of her halting oration, calls to mind Socrates' speech in Plato's *Symposium*. Repeating the words of his female mentor, Diotima (the only female perspective offered in *The Symposium*), Socrates claims that "the object of love is not beauty" but rather "birth and procreation in a beautiful medium."[55] Procreation does not, for Diotima, have to refer to the birth of physical children; it can also result in the birth of "virtue, and especially wisdom."[56] Diotima explicitly describes love as a form of continuity:

> Why procreation? Because procreation is as close as a mortal can get to being immortal and undying. Given our agreement that the aim of love is the permanent possession of goodness for oneself, it necessarily follows that we desire immortality along with goodness, and consequently the aim of love has to be immortality as well.[57]

Woolf, through Peggy, seems to be taking an even stricter tack than Diotima, for, in her symposium, neither physical procreation nor intellectual creation is sufficient to ensure happiness (as eudemonia) or "a livable world" (to cite Butler). Perhaps the concept of beauty, so undone by the monstrous chimeric drawing that incited Peggy's speech, needs to be re-envisioned, or procreation – which needs to take place "in a beautiful medium," as Diotima suggests – cannot take place in "a world bursting with misery ... or worse – tyranny; brutality; torture; the fall of civilization; the end of freedom" (TY 388). In either case, the norm has grown freakish by the end of *The Years*. This is not the ending, however, for Woolf seems to suggest that such a recognition is a starting place for a new way of perceiving the richness of "living differently" (TY 391). For that reason, the novel ends not with Peggy's agonized call to live differently, but with an allusion to the sun cycle that shapes the interludes of *The Waves*. The last scene belongs to Eleanor, who, from a Platonic point of view, is not as barren as North (thinking only of marriage and childbearing), imagines her to be. Turning to her siblings as the party ends:

> "And now?" she said, looking at Morris, who was drinking the last drops of a glass of wine. "And now?" she asked, holding out her hands to him."
>
> The sun had risen, and the sky above the houses wore an air of extraordinary beauty, simplicity and peace. (435)

This ending, coming so soon after Peggy's anti-normative outburst, gently but firmly pries the fissures in heteronormative ideology open further, ending with siblings rather than procreative couples, expanding beyond the family (already expanded beyond biological kin in the large, intergenerational gathering that Eleanor is now leaving), and leaving the readers with the image of open air – signifying for Woolf a "freedom from unreal loyalties."[58]

The sprawling gathering highlights the characters' interdependence, but not without the specter of precarity ushering them out the door (into the open air). Just before the guests leave, Delia, the Pargiter sister who has hosted the party, brings the two children of the caretaker up to the drawing room to give them each a piece of cake. They become something of a spectacle for the middle- and upper-middle-class partygoers: "They looked awkward and clumsy" in front of the guests, and "frightened" as the hostess commands them to eat (TY 428–29). None of the partygoers can understand the cockney accent with which the two children sing as the behest of Martin, who has essentially bribed the children out of their silent staring by asking them to "sing a song for sixpence!" (TY 429). This penultimate scene hearkens back to the epistemic arrogance that Woolf counters in *Three Guineas*, the sister text to *The Years*, as the privileged partygoers have no impetus to understand cockney speakers from the working class, although the working class must necessarily understand the language of the middle and upper classes in order to exist as laborers. Perhaps for this reason the children are addressed primarily in imperatives such as "Eat!" "Speak!" and "Sing!" (TY 429). Considered together as twin aspects of the novel's ending, this scene of precarity amidst a scene of interdependence makes Eleanor's question "And now?" a gesture signifying a fragile but perceptible futurity.

# 4 Civilization and Barbarism: A Reparative Exegesis

It is perhaps impossible to write the word "civilization" in the context of modernist literary expression without conjuring up the image of Joseph Conrad's Mr. Kurtz imploring Marlow to safeguard his supposedly altruistic report for "The International Society for the Suppression of Savage Customs,'" on which he has scribbled "Exterminate all the brutes!" in a fit of delirious self-recognition.[1] As Porter Abbott notes, "All rivers in early twentieth-century fiction are not necessarily fed by the great river in *Heart of Darkness*, but Conrad's vexed rendering of the classic male story of penetration had a lasting impact on the figuration of narrative."[2] In addition to convoluting the traditional narrative of exploration and discovery, Conrad's tale exposes the "civilizing" mission of European colonizers as an alibi for economic exploitation and brute conquest. As Walter Benjamin suggests, "There is no document of civilization that is not at the same time a document of barbarism. And just as such a document is not free of barbarism, barbarism taints also the manner in which it was transmitted from one owner to another."[3] Woolf's oeuvre is not immune to the force of Benjamin's insight. Alongside (or, more precisely, embedded within) her cogent critiques of colonialism, fascism, and sexism are troubling, ethically indigestible references to marginalized others – persons with cognitive disabilities (as I noted in Chapter 3) and ethnic and racial others (from "natives ... so beautiful ... half naked" to a "very fine negress," to stereotypically portrayed Jews, Gypsies, and Turks, among others).[4]

It is important to register these moments in Woolf's work – that is, to be humbly honest about the aspects of Woolf's prose that disappoint and hurt. Pointing these moments out, however, is not the end of critical reading, but rather the beginning of a process of critical questioning and discussion – a practice that Woolf herself advocated in her 1934 essay, "Why?" In that essay for Somerville College's literary magazine, *Lysistrata*, Woolf not only asks the question "why?" repeatedly, but also questions how knowledge is formed and disseminated. "Know?" her fictional interlocutor in the essay asks, "What d'you mean by 'know'?"[5] Woolf's questions are intended to be followed by discussion, not authoritative answer. "Why not bring together people of all ages and both sexes and all shades of fame and obscurity so that they can talk, without mounting platforms or reading papers or wearing expensive clothes or eating expensive food?" Woolf asks.[6] "Why not invent human intercourse? Why not try?"[7] Such a practice moves beyond the "obsolete custom" of lecturing (which, for Woolf, can take place on the podium or in print).[8] Moreover, Woolf's suggested practice of relentlessly asking questions and *staying for the answers* opens up a space for what Eve Kosofsky Sedgwick calls "reparative reading" – a practice that is both vulnerable and ethical, open to surprise (both pleasurable surprise and painful) and oriented toward "the often very fragile concern to provide the self with pleasure and nourishment in an environment that is perceived as not particularly offering them."[9]

"Reparative reading," which Sedgwick aligns with Melanie Klein's "depressive position," offers an alternative to what Sedgwick calls "a paranoid critical stance" – a mode of literary and cultural criticism where ideologically suspect moves and motives in a text are "unveiled."[10] While Sedgwick uses the term "paranoid" in the specific context of Silvan Thompkins' study of affect, I prefer her less loaded term, "unveiling," as it is less likely to imply, however unintentionally, that a critical reading of the ideological underpinnings of a text is faulty or unwarranted.[11] Sedgwick is quick to clarify that a "paranoid" affective stance is perfectly reasonable in a culture where "no one need be delusional to find evidence of systematic oppression," but she argues nevertheless that there may be value in other methods and modes of reading as well. "I myself have no wish to return to the use of 'paranoid' as a pathologizing diagnosis," Sedgwick notes, "but it seems to me a great loss when paranoid inquiry comes to seem entirely coextensive with critical theoretical inquiry rather than being viewed as one kind of cognitive/affective theoretical practice among other, alternative kinds."[12] The unveiling impetus in critical practice is not mistaken or off-target, then, but, in Sedgwick's view, its very success as a "strong" methodology "may have made it less rather than more possible to unpack the local, contingent relations between any given piece of knowledge and its narrative/epistemological entailments for the seeker, knower, or teller."[13]

The kind of "unpacking" "seek[ing]," "know[ing]," and "tell [ing]" that Sedgwick advocates is liable to appear "naïve" or "complaisant" because, as Sedgwick argues, "The vocabulary for articulating any reader's reparative motive toward a text or a culture has long been so sappy, aestheticizing, defensive, anti-intellectual, or reactionary that it's no wonder few critics are willing to describe their acquaintance with such motives."[14] The last several decades of Woolf scholarship has not tended toward the "anti-intellectual, or reactionary," and, given Woolf's aesthetic achievements, it is very difficult to find fault with an aesthetic appreciation for her work. Arguably, most of the "sappy" recuperations of Woolf appear in pop culture rather than Woolf scholarship, at least if the myriad Woolf plush dolls, handbags, finger puppets, T-shirts, mugs, and posters are taken as evidence.[15] The temptation to defensively explain away Woolf's problematic remarks or practices, however, is a strong one, still. The challenge for Woolf readers today, then, is to read "reparatively" without reading defensively. "The reparative reading position," Sedgwick explains, "undertakes a different range of affects, ambitions, and risks. What we can best learn from such practices are, perhaps, the many ways selves and communities succeed in extracting sustenance from the objects of a culture – even of a culture whose avowed desire has often been not to sustain them."[16] For this reason there is value in reading Woolf reparatively (and reading Woolf herself as engaged in reparative reading) despite the risks – which include vulnerability to surprise and openness to failure – because such a stance provides insight into how (or why, to ask Woolf's question) her oeuvre is simultaneously a "document of civilization" and an indicator of "barbarism," and how (or why) that barbarism and civilization are transmitted.[17]

## "WHAT IS THIS 'CIVILIZATION' IN WHICH WE FIND OURSELVES?"[18]

To address these questions, it is necessary to revisit the terms "barbarism" and "civilization" as they are typically used in liberal democratic rhetoric, a rhetoric that was cultivated, ironically, in "the age of empire."[19] Benjamin himself revalues these terms by suggesting that they are inextricable, operating as different sides of the same coin. That is, Benjamin links "civilization" directly to originary violence, a concept attributable to Ernst Renan's remarks on the founding of nations: "Historical inquiry, in effect, throws light on the violent acts that have taken place at the origin of every political formation, even those that have been the most benevolent in their consequences. Unity is always brutally established."[20] Commenting on Benjamin's "Critique of Violence," Ari Hirvonen explains that "For Benjamin, violence is immanently and inextricably present in modern law – in the legal norms, practices, and institutions."[21] Founding violence – for example, a military invasion of a geographic area deemed in need of "civilizing" – masks itself as "law positing violence." Such violence, Hirvonen explains, "is thus not pure and immediate violence but instrumental and mediated violence used in the name of posited law, which will, after the fact, legitimize it."[22] In other words, founding violence is redescribed as creation – the "birth" of civilization, of law and order – and the violence committed both to bring about this order and to maintain it is retroactively justified in the name of civilization. Revaluing the terms "civilization" and "barbarism" thus entails undoing the work of redescription that aligns "civilization" with the violent imposition of power onto others, and considers "barbaric" all of those who have been marginalized by that imposition of power and chafe at its enforcement. Thus, to return to Benjamin's thesis on the inextricability of "barbarism" and "civilization," barbarism is not banished by the hallmarks of civilization. Rather, disguised as law and custom, barbarism (the brute force of the law and the violence of conquest) props up the dominant cultural civilization. (This last insight is, indeed, a "paranoid" reading according to

Sedgwick's criteria, but she never does suggest that we do away with this method of reading altogether.)

Jane Marcus scrutinizes the "taint" (to use Benjamin's term) of this form of barbarism in Woolf's otherwise progressive work in an extended reading of the following passage from *A Room of One's Own*:

> And of course, it may not be a dog [that men want to possess], I thought, remembering Parliament Square, the Sieges Allee and other avenues; it may be a piece of land or a man with curly black hair. It is one of the great advantages of being woman that one can pass even a very fine negress without wishing to make an Englishwoman of her.[23]

Reading the passage in the context of Woolf's great grandfather James Stephen's efforts to abolish slavery in the British Empire, Marcus suggests that the otherness of Blackness, for Woolf, forestalls the full potential of her critique of imperialism, patriarchy, and acquisitive capitalism:

> The text is marked by the guilty admission that the narrator's five hundred pounds a year comes from an aunt who died from a fall while taking the night air in Bombay. Woolf's generation of Englishwomen writes, she is saying, with the blood of the nineteenth-century imperialists on their hands. The assumption that a Negress must be a foreigner or colonial subject was an excuse for ignoring the presence in Britain of blacks in goodly numbers for centuries.[24]

In Marcus's reading, Woolf is simultaneously anti-imperialist – mocking what she sees as a primarily male desire to possess other people's land and, more appallingly, other people – and unaware (perhaps due to "epistemic arrogance") about the existence of Afro-British subjects of her own nation. While Afro-British Londoners represented a minority of the population, research by Caroline Bressey at the Equiano Center of the University College London indicates that there were a number of Black artists and intellectuals active in late Victorian London, including John Alcindor, a founder of the African Progress Union, and composer Samuel Coleridge-Taylor.[25] Just a few years after Woolf published *A Room of One's Own*, Black Trinidadian writer and theorist C. L. R. James moved to London and, although not generally considered a main figure in the Bloomsbury group, he did publish *The Case for West-Indian Self Government* with the Woolfs' Hogarth Press in 1933.[26] The Hogarth Press also published *An African Speaks for His People* in 1934.[27]

Despite Woolf's rational awareness of Black Londoners, as well as of the ravages of empire and racism on African people, Black subjects were nevertheless largely figurative for Woolf – that is, they were not depicted as actual persons with a full range of human subjectivities, personalities, and interests. Such is indicated by her casual use of the "N-word" as the tenor in similes about hard work or sun exposure. In *The Years*, for example, Eleanor exclaims, "What a gipsy I look! . . . Burnt brown as a nigger!" (TY 343). In *Between the Acts*, the narration describes Miss La Trobe as "work[ing] like a nigger" (BTA 150). Woolf uses the word in her diary as well, so it is not simply the case that she is deploying it to expose her characters' chauvinism, as is the case in her depiction of the young nobleman "slicing at the head of a Moor" in *Orlando's* first description of its protagonist (O 11). In her April 15, 1920 diary entry, for example, Woolf notes, "The day before I went to the Niggers' show in Chelsea; very sad impressive figures; obscene; somehow monumental; figures of Frenchmen, I thought, sodden with civilisation & cynicism; yet they were carved (perhaps) in the Congo 100's of years ago."[28] One could debate the relative offensiveness of the "N-word" in 1930s England – that is, whether or not it was as offensive there and then as it is here and now – but such a discussion would merely elaborate relative *degrees* of radical othering. Whether we take her use of the term as a merely unfortunate deployment of the vocabulary of her era, a distasteful glimpse into her white privilege, or an extremely offensive sign of explicit racism, the point still remains that for Woolf, people of African origin, when mentioned at all, generally serve as metaphorical figures rather than as actual people.

In the face of such evidence – which, to be fair, can be dredged up against most, if not all, white modernists – the lure of defensive reading is strong. Woolf *was* of her time, and, as Helen Carr notes, in a careful essay on Woolf's engagement with issues of empire and race,

Attitudes absorbed in childhood are hard to escape fully, even when consciously and intellectually rejected. [Woolf] certainly struggled with her own anti-Semitism. Her anti-imperialism has to be understood in terms of its

time, when among many intellectuals and modernists the nineteenth-century assumption of western, European superiority was coming under scrutiny in many ways, and yet all the same attitudes to other races were
changing very slowly.[29]

In a reparative, rather than a defensive reading, Woolf's being "of her
time" is neither an excuse nor a smoking gun to unveil. Rather, her
position as a white, relatively privileged Englishwoman is part of the
interpretive landscape of her work that requires (to return to
Murdoch's insights) "careful and just *attention*."[30]

Reading *To the Lighthouse* in conjunction with Woolf's 1906
Constantinople diaries, for example, Urmila Seshagiri argues that the
concept of racial difference underpins much of Woolf's aesthetic practice, even when the ostensible subject is gender difference or colonial
exploitation. "The 'question of the West & the East,'" explains
Seshagiri, "infiltrates many of Woolf's major works, transforming
Englishness and modernity into sites defined by racial difference,
imperialism, and Orientalism."[31] In that diary, written when Woolf
(then Virginia Stephen) was twenty-four, Woolf notes that "The only
remark I can make with any confidence is that no Christian, or even
European, can hope to understand the Turkish point of view; you are
born Christians or Mahommedans [*sic*] as surely as you are born black
or white."[32] Having penned this ostensible fact of difference "in the
blood that beats in the pulse," Woolf then troubles the imperialist
viewpoint one might expect to follow from these words, remarking
that "We gazed as we might have gazed at creatures behind a cage; only
the truth was that these creatures were neither our captives nor our
inferiors; they suffered us to watch them, but they would not suffer us
to pray with them."[33]

Focusing on how Woolf troubles the imperialist gaze, rather
than how she aesthetically deploys "racial difference, imperialism,
and Orientalism," other scholars such as Melba Cuddy-Keane and
Jeanne Dubino read Woolf's 1906 diary as advancing more reflec-
tive and self-conscious ideas regarding racial and religious
difference.[34] Reading her diary alongside a short story, "A
Dialogue upon Mount Pentelicus," embedded in that diary,
Dubino balances Woolf's "lingering orientalism" against her

critique of British chauvinism, arguing that "Woolf had earlier in the story mocked the Englishmen for another kind of orientalizing – namely, for their denouncing the 'escort of dirty Greek peasant boys' as '"barbarians"' for failing to understand their Harrow-inflected ancient Greek, and for convicting the entire people as a 'spurious, ... dusky garrulous race.'"[35] Cuddy-Keane reads Woolf's writing in general as a rhetorical model of "a way of speaking with others that allows space for diversities in fundamental paradigms of thought."[36] She cites the same diary passage that, for Seshagiri, indicated Woolf's aesthetic reliance on racial difference, as an example of Woolf's dialogic rhetorical practice: "The influence of experiencing other cultures is evident in Woolf's early travel diaries, where she avoids the inscription of cultural binaries by refusing to define the other in her own terms: 'when we come to consider the question of the West & the East – then indeed – we lay down the pen, & write no more.'"[37]

Both of these insights – that Woolf reinscribes racial and cultural difference, that Woolf interrogates ideologies of racial and cultural difference – might be simultaneously true. Kathy Phillips, for example, argues that Woolf's work as a whole is consistently anti-imperialist:

> Colonies such as Morocco, coveted territories such as Venezuela, and apologists for Empire such as Sir Edward Grey form an insistent bass note in Woolf's novels. She had a detailed knowledge of colonialism, derived particularly from her husband Leonard Woolf's writings on imperialism and international government. When his *Empire and Commerce in Africa* was published in January 1920, she reported, "I'm reading it for the second time – to me it seems superb" (*Letters* 2: 413). In fact, in summer 1917 she had helped with the research for this book.[38]

It is possible that Woolf maintained a theoretical objection to colonialism without fully examining the influence of imperialism's ideological export – racism – on her own psyche as a privileged white Englishwoman. Phillips suggests as much, contending that "Despite Virginia Woolf's residual insensitivity to colonized people and her lack of first-hand knowledge of the colonies, she felt strongly that the English civilization which the British imposed on their subjects was not worth exporting."[39]

On the other hand, Woolf, like her husband Leonard, was deeply invested in preserving a form of civilization with strong cosmopolitan, human rights, and anti-imperialist elements. As Christine Froula notes in *Virginia Woolf and the Bloomsbury Avant-Garde*, Bloomsbury thinkers were preoccupied with the cultivation and maintenance of civilization in the face of pressure from "barbarians" both inside and outside of British culture:

> As the 1914 war plunged Europe into crisis, as belligerent nationalisms (even in England) and rising totalitarianisms threatened to eclipse Europe's Enlightenment ideal, Bloomsbury artists and intellectuals entered a struggle not to "save" their civilization but to help advance Europe toward its own unrealized ideal, a civilization that had never existed. Bloomsbury carries the Enlightenment struggle for civilization dialectically into the twentieth century in its pacifism and internationalism, its sense of history not as inevitable progress but as an unending fight for a future that is always open and free, and – most tellingly – its address to barbarity within Europe and the West.[40]

Leonard Woolf, who published his antifascist political treatise *Barbarians at the Gate* in 1939, locates "barbarism" in Europe, and defines it in terms of political or communal actions. Describing a shift in consciousness from pre–World War I European expectations of civil society to contemporary (i.e., circa 1939) expectations of civil society, he writes, "When you opened your newspaper in those days [before the Great War], you did not read of the wholesale torture, persecution, expropriation, imprisonment or liquidation of tens of thousands or hundreds of thousands of persons, classified or labeled for destruction as social democrats, Communists, Jews, Lutheran pastors, Roman Catholics, capitalists, or kulaks."[41] Inverting the fascist insistence on race or ethnicity as a marker of one's barbarity or civilized status, Leonard Woolf defines barbarism and civilization as performative, or characterized by doing, rather than ontological, or characterized by being (who one is, "barbaric" or "civilized," by virtue of race or nation or tribe).[42] In simple terms, in order to *be* civilized, one must act in a civilized manner regardless of education, race, class, or nation. The brutalities of World War I reinforced for Leonard and Virginia Woolf, as well as their Bloomsbury comrades, the lesson that neither geographical location, nor national belonging, nor race, nor complexity of artistic, educational, or scientific achievements guaranteed that one's people would act in a "civilized" way.

Moreover, for Leonard Woolf the performative "doing" of civilization depends on communal action rather than individual characteristics:

> The knowledge which is relevant to barbarism and civilization is knowledge which determines communal action (e.g., encouragement or prohibition of human sacrifice), social behavior, or the general economic conditions of a community. The reason is that civilization is a quality of societies or of individuals in their social relations. Only those true or false beliefs therefore affect it which affect communal action, social organization, economic conditions, or the behavior of individuals to other human beings.[43]

One might reasonably ask, what is "knowledge which determines communal action?" For Leonard Woolf, such "civilization consists partly in facts which [are] acts and partly in facts which [are] thoughts, beliefs, aims, intentions, and ideals."[44] Putting these two insights together, commonly held values – or what we could call dominant discourses (e.g., "thoughts, beliefs, aims, intentions and ideals") – fuel communal action, social and economic organization, and interpersonal behaviors. These commonly held values are shaped by culture (the fine arts and literature, as well as popular culture), by "memory and tradition," by education, and by ideology or what Virginia Woolf calls "atmosphere."[45] The writer, the artist, the educator, and the critic thus all contribute to shaping and reshaping the "thoughts, beliefs, aims, intentions and ideals" that move a community or society to act. They pave the way for civilization, or, conversely, barbarism.

SAW-TOOTHED SOCIETY

In August of 1924, in the midst of writing *Mrs. Dalloway*, Woolf was asked to write a lead essay for the *Times Literary Supplement* on the death of Joseph Conrad.[46] Woolf's appreciation of Conrad was nuanced, beginning with a scintillating tribute to the beauty of his prose:

> One opens his pages and feels as Helen must have felt when she looked in her glass and realised that, do what she would, she could never in any

circumstances pass for a plain woman. So Conrad had been gifted, so he had schooled himself ... that it seemed impossible for him to make an ugly or insignificant movement of the pen.[47]

Assessing his significance as a novelist further, Woolf detects a form of moral courage in Conrad's wrestling with ambivalence and ambiguity in character development, suggesting that he refused to be false, and therefore penned his characters with an almost agonizing reticence born of exactitude:

> For the vision of a novelist is both complex and specialised; complex, because behind his characters and apart from them must stand something stable to which he relates them; specialised because since he is a single person with one sensibility the aspects of life in which he can believe with conviction are strictly limited. So delicate a balance is easily disturbed ... When he had to indicate their relation to that other unseen world of novelists, the world of values and convictions, he was far less sure what those values were. Then, over and over again, a single phrase, "He steered with care", coming at the end of a storm, carried in it a whole morality.[48]

Woolf's affinity for Conrad is not accidental, for her vision, too, is complex and specialized, balanced delicately. It is no surprise to find, then, that literary critics have found intertextual allusions to Conrad in her fiction, especially her first and last novels, *The Voyage Out* and *Between the Acts*.[49]

Kathy Phillips comments on the geographical similarity between *The Voyage Out*'s river voyage to a remote colonial outpost in South America and Marlow's river voyage to a colonial outpost in the Belgian Congo in *Heart of Darkness*. "Some critics suggest that Woolf may have borrowed the river trip from Joseph Conrad's *Heart of Darkness*," she writes,

> but they assume she avoids Conrad's attention to European exploitation of foreign countries, to concentrate instead on one woman's personal problems ... My reading of *The Voyage Out* reverses these conclusions ... Far from neglecting Conrad's setting in a European colony, Woolf extends his investigation of the effects of commerce and colonization and condemns them even more scathingly than he.[50]

Conrad's *Heart of Darkness* sets a very high bar for scathing critiques of European colonialism, and it is not clear that *The Voyage Out*, with its subtle unraveling of the Jane Austen marriage plot (relocated from

Bath to Santa Marina) meets that bar. Nevertheless, the novel does cast a withering gaze on the trappings of British "civilization," which appear superficial and foundationless when they are taken out of their usual setting and transported to another country, climate, and culture. In her analysis of *British Fiction and Cross-Cultural Encounters*, Carey J. Snyder describes this gaze as "self-nativizing," a term attributed to anthropologist Clifford Geertz indicating one's "turning an ethnographic eye back on the home culture and using 'extravagant otherness' as a means of 'self-critique.'"[51]

The novel's first description of San Marina does contain an element of self-critique, reading like a satirical sketch in *Punch:*

> The Spaniards, bloated with fine living upon the fruits of the miraculous land, fell in heaps; but the hardy Englishmen, tawny with sea-voyaging, hairy for lack of razors, with muscles like wire, fangs greedy for flesh, and fingers itching for gold, despatched and wounded, drove the dying into the sea, and soon reduced the natives to a state of superstitious wonderment. Here a settlement was made; women were imported; children grew. All seemed to favor the expansion of the British Empire, and had there been men like Richard Dalloway in the time of Charles the First, the map would undoubtedly be red where it is now an odious green. (VO 89)

This brief sketch of English colonial history is narrated without attribution to a particular character, but the entire sketch is marked as "the piece of information that died within [Mr. Pepper]" because no one took him up on his professorial preamble to a disquisition:

> "Three hundred years odd," said Mr. Pepper meditatively at length.
> As nobody said "What?" he merely extracted a bottle and swallowed a pill. The piece of information that died within him was to the effect that three hundred years ago five Elizabethan barques had anchored where the *Euphrosyne* now floated. (VO 88)

The lengthy "history" (a tale of founding violence) that follows Mr. Pepper's pill popping thus provides insight into British chauvinism of the type that a scholar such as Pepper might hold. The tale's reference to the "odious green" and "red" of the map is a direct allusion to *Heart of Darkness* and Marlow's description of a color-coded map in a Belgian imperial expedition office, with each colonial "possession" denoted by colors of the homeland:

[O]n one end a large shining map, marked with all the colours of a rainbow. There was a vast amount of red – good to see at any time, because one knows that some real work is done in there, a deuce of a lot of blue, a little green, smears of orange, and, on the East Coast, a purple patch, to show where the jolly pioneers of progress drink the jolly lager-beer.[52]

The game-like portrayal of the map – with its colors divvying up the spoils of colonial competition – coupled with the boys'-adventure-story style of the story of Santa Marina's founding (featuring the hardy British sailors walloping the drunken "bloated" Spaniards) sets the scene for much of the action undertaken by the English tourist community in Santa Marina. Aside from Mr. Ambrose, who spends his time editing Pindar, and Miss Allan, who is writing a *Primer of English Literature*, most of the English travelers fill their time with games – bridge, chess, tennis – and social gatherings – picnics, dances, meals, and excursions.

This form of "society" resembles Woolf's description of the late Victorian society that she and her sister Vanessa were subjected to as young women (much like the protagonist of *The Voyage Out*, Rachel Vinrace). Describing a typical day for her and Vanessa in 1900, Woolf writes, "Society – upper middle class Victorian society – came into being when the lights went up. About seven thirty the pressure of the machine became emphatic."[53] Comparing her father Leslie Stephen's "Victorian code" with her half-brother George's less principled and more status-conscious adherence to social norms, Woolf explains:

But if father had the lager lines of the age stamped into him, George filled them in with a crisscross, with a crowquill etching of the most minute details. No more perfect fossil of the Victorian age could exist. And so, while father preserved the framework of 1860, George filled in the frame-work with all kinds of minutely-teethed saws; and the machine into which our rebellious bodies were inserted in 1900 not only held us tight in its framework, but bit into us with innumerable sharp teeth.[54]

Similar "sharp teeth" trap and kill Rachel Vinrace, who cannot or will not survive the relentless drive of the marriage plot. She contracts a fever shortly after her engagement to Terrence Hewett and a myster-ious tumble in the grass with him (and her Aunt playing the part of the Austenian chaperone) in the wilds of a jungle clearing (VO 283). The British tourists attribute Rachel's death to the supposedly primitive conditions around them. "'That's the worst of these places,' [Mr. Flushing] said. 'People will behave as though they are in England and they are not. I've no doubt myself that Miss Vinrace caught the infection up at the villa itself. She probably ran risks a dozen times a day that might have given her an illness'" (VO 359). Turning the mirror back onto the British chauvinism of the tourists, one could suggest that the malady is precisely that "people will behave as though they are in England," and that behavior leaves an Austenian heroine little space to flourish outside of the normative marriage plot which ends most stories. For that reason, it is significant (as I mention in Chapter 1) that the novel ends not with Rachel's death, but with Evelyn's flight from a proposal of marriage to adventure and, perhaps, aretē.

### A REPARATIVE IMPERATIVE

Building on the subtler, intertextual critique of English "civilization" in *The Voyage Out*, Woolf develops a more forceful criticism of the propensity of dominant powers (especially colonialist ones) to commit acts of atrocity in the name of civilization in her extended essays *A Room of One's Own* and *Three Guineas*. In *Room*, she explains the logic of cultural dominance with an extended conceit, figuring women as "looking-glasses possessing the magic and delicious power of reflecting the figure of man at twice its natural size" (AROO 35). Not without irony, for the "barbarism" of conquest appears as the precursor to nation and culture building, Woolf suggests that this looking-glass distortion was necessary for "civilization" to have developed:

> Life for both sexes – and I looked at them, shouldering their way along the pavement – is arduous, difficult, a perpetual struggle. It calls for gigantic courage and strength. More than anything, perhaps, creatures of illusion as we are, it calls for confidence in oneself. Without self-confidence we are as babes in the cradle. And how can we generate this imponderable quality, which is yet so invaluable, most quickly? By thinking that other people are inferior to one self ... Hence the enormous importance to a patriarch who has

to conquer, who has to rule, of feeling that great numbers of people, half the
human race indeed, are by nature inferior to himself. (AROO 35)

Without the power of the looking-glass's self-aggrandizing reflection,
Woolf continues, "probably the earth would still be swamp and jungle" (AROO 35).

Woolf's double-sided depictions of "civilization" appear as well
in *Mrs. Dalloway*, when Peter Walsh, recently arrived in London from
his colonial service in India, sees the ambulance heading toward the
corpse of Septimus Smith (who cannot be said to have survived his
service to King and Country) and smugly muses that it is "One of the
triumphs of civilization" (Mrs. D 151). Janice Ho reads the appearance
of the ambulance in *Mrs. Dalloway* as indicating the increasing rele-
vance of "social citizenship" in a British culture transitioning from
the predominance of liberal individualist ideology to an ideology of
"social liberalism" that culminated in the post–World War II welfare
state.[55] Attributing Peter Walsh's sentiments to Woolf herself, Ho
argues that:

> Woolf's description of the ambulance as simultaneously "communal" and
> "humane," "efficien[t]," "clean," and "organis[ed]" invokes the diverse and
> ambivalent ideological rationales underpinning the practices of social
> reform in this era: if these were justifiable through a progressive liberal
> politics that emphasized collective good and the welfare of the people, they
> could also be supported by more conservative agendas of nationalism and
> imperialism concerned with social engineering and national greatness.[56]

Ho's own analysis of the "diverse and ambivalent ideological ratio-
nales" interwoven in social liberalism reinforces Benjamin's point
that civilization and barbarism are two sides of the same coin. In
this instance, although the ambulance is a marker of seeming communal care, Peter Walsh's pride in this appearance of the ambulance is
made possible by his forgetting (or perhaps Britain's communal forgetting) of the other scenes an ambulance might evoke so soon after
the end of World War I. That is, the figure of the ambulance is just as
likely to evoke (for those who experienced the war closer to home than
Walsh did) the ambulances which transported those wounded at the
front to hospitals and aid stations where medical technology (also a
barometer of "civilization") might, or might not, heal them. Peter has

the luxury, or privilege, of escaping that memory, but, through its depiction of Septimus Smith, the novel makes clear that others might be more likely to associate the ambulance with the carnage of a barbaric war than with the benefits of civilization. This difference is one of perspective and context, rather than inherent in the figure of the ambulance, which is simultaneously a marker of civilization and a reminder of barbarism.

In a similar fashion, other markers of civilization are double-edged in *Mrs. Dalloway*, as reminders of the cost of social reform – the exclusion of those unfit or deemed unworthy of the attention of the benevolent state – percolate just beneath the surface of the ordered streets and fine parties of Mrs. Dalloway's social set. Social pillar Lady Bruton, for example, is concocting a scheme to emigrate presumably unemployed young English people to Canada for a fresh start during a period of growing labor unrest in Britain (Mrs. D 108). While this benevolent action is undertaken, as Ho suggests, from a conviction that the state has a responsibility for the social welfare of its citizens, the novel makes clear that Lady Bruton's program would be under-taken on behalf of "young people of both sexes born of respectable parents" – that is, subjects deserving of the state's attention (Mrs. D 106).[57] The plight of young people born of less-than-respectable par-ents is apparently of no consequence to Lady Bruton, who, like the figures of men magnified by the distortion of female "looking glasses" in *A Room of One's Own*, is enhanced by the "inevitably prismatic, lustrous, half looking-glass, half precious stone" qualities of her ben-evolent social reform schemes (Mrs. D 106).

Richard Dalloway, meanwhile, sits on a parliamentary commit-tee to discuss the Armenian genocide, although Clarissa Dalloway is nonchalant (confusing the Armenians with the Albanians) about an event that was, in 1915, an extreme example of human brutality:

> She cared much more for her roses than for the Armenians. Hunted out of existence, maimed, frozen, the victims of cruelty and injustice (she had heard Richard say so over and over again) – no, she could feel nothing for the Albanians, or was it the Armenians? but she loved her roses (didn't that help the Armenians?) – the only flowers she could bear to see cut. [58] (Mrs. D 120)

How we read this scene depends on how we view Woolf, and vice versa. In the spirit of Benjamin's epigram – "There is no document of civilization that is not at the same time a document of barbarism" – we can read the barbarism and brutality of World War I as well as the Armenian genocide as the flip side of the story of British "civilization," represented by the high-society party that takes place on the day of Septimus's suicide. Although magnificent in its splendor, the party's juxtaposition with death (Septimus), displacement (unemployed ex-soldiers being shipped off to Canada), and exclusion (Rezia Warren Smith; Miss Kilman) suggests that "civilization" has its costs.

Claiming that Woolf might be somewhat critical of Mrs. Dalloway's party, while admiring it for its flair, runs counter to late-twentieth-century pop-cultural depictions of Woolf, which tend to envision her as a Clarissa Dalloway double rather as someone who might find Clarissa's nonchalance about matters of human rights and social justice problematic. The imagery of Marleen Goris's 1997 film of *Mrs. Dalloway*, starring Vanessa Redgrave and Natascha McElhone, is just one symptom of this phenomenon. The implied equivalence is unmistakable in the iconography of the film. McElhone wears her hair in a style very similar to Woolf's 1902 Beresford photo, and in one scene is dressed and made up to look very much like a Stephen sister, if not Virginia Woolf herself. The older Clarissa, played by Vanessa Redgrave, also wears her hair and holds her head in a manner suggested by photos of Woolf, this time by Gisèle Freund, who photographed Woolf when she was 57. Redgrave's dress is seemingly more appropriate for evening and her makeup more elaborate than Woolf's, but the resemblance is nonetheless suggestive.

While these likenesses do not make an argument (to borrow a phrase from *Three Guineas*), they do suggest a persistent temptation in Woolf studies and pop culture alike to conflate the author with her works or her characters, for better (and who would not want to be played by Vanessa Redgrave?) or worse (TG 14). Brenda Silver analyzes this phenomenon in her magnificent study of more than 35 years of Woolf imagery in Anglo/American culture – *Virginia Woolf: Icon*. "Occurring across the cultural terrain, whether in academic discourses, the intellectual media or mass/popular culture," Silver argues, "the proliferation of Virginia Woolfs has transformed the writer into a powerful and powerfully contested cultural icon, whose name, face, and authority are persistently claimed or disclaimed in debates about art, politics, sexuality, gender, class, the 'canon,' fashion, feminism, race, and anger."[59] For Silver, the icon of Woolf has become a symbol that exceeds and often overshadows her status as an author and a public intellectual. It is possible that more people know her now from mugs, posters, and filmic representations than they do from reading her books.

As I mention in the Introduction to this book, a favorite motif for Woolf is the image of "open air," unclouded by cultural impediments – a metaphor for the ability to think for one's self without pressure from outside influences. Woolf most famously references the open air in *A Room of One's Own*, when the narrator's legacy from an aunt "unveiled the sky to me and substituted for the large and imposing figure of a gentleman, which Milton recommended for my perpetual adoration, a view of the open sky" (39). It may not be possible to clear the air of the myriad Virginia Woolf images cluttering our visual landscape, many of them representing unpleasant facts about her (she was, at times, a snob; she maintained conscious and unconscious jealous rivalries with contemporary female writers; she often wrote stinging comments about others in her diary; and she benefitted from the spoils of empire and the fruits of capitalism even as she critiqued them). It is nevertheless worth the effort to read Woolf's expansive oeuvre with open eyes – reparatively, that is – so that the insights that she can offer us are not lost in the shadow of her icons.

Reparative reading does not mean dismissing one's knowledge that symbolic systems, such as British literature, participate in dominant discourses (or the discourses of domination). Rather, reparative reading involves making oneself open (and thus vulnerable) to the possibility that a work might emanate a force or meaning that cannot be predicted in advance of the experience. As Sedgwick explains:

> [T]o read from a reparative position is to surrender the knowing, anxious paranoid determination that no horror, however apparently unthinkable, shall ever come to the reader as new; to a reparatively positioned reader, it

can seem realistic and necessary to experience surprise. Because there can be terrible surprises, however, there can also be good ones. Hope, often a fracturing, even a traumatic thing to experience, is among the energies by which the reparatively positioned reader tries to organize the fragments and part-objects she encounters or creates. Because the reader has room to realize that the future may be different from the present, it is also possible for her to entertain such profoundly painful, profoundly relieving, ethically crucial possibilities as that the past, in turn, could have happened differently from the way it actually did.[60]

Woolf herself is amenable to the possibility that one can, from the perspective of a "profoundly painful" moment in the present, imagine how history might have been lived differently to arrive at a different conclusion with a more livable future. Her hypothetical experimental college, where civilization would be fostered by providing the means to "explore the ways in which the mind and body can be made to co-operate; discover what new combinations make good wholes in human life" is one such imagining – taking place, not coincidentally, on the eve of World War II (TG 43).

If we read *Three Guineas* as a reparative reading (i.e., if we do not simply read *Three Guineas* reparatively, but as *itself* a reparative reading of European civilization at a moment of intense precarity), then Woolf's essay is much more than a witty critique of British and European hypocrisy. It is a call to action – the action of thinking:

Let us think in offices; in omnibuses; while we are standing in the crowd watching Coronations and Lord Mayor's Shows; let us think as we pass the Cenotaph; and in Whitehall; in the gallery of the House of Commons; in the Law Courts; let us think at baptisms and marriages and funerals. Let us never cease from thinking – what is this "civilization" in which we find ourselves? What are these ceremonies and why should we take part in them? (TG 77)

Woolf provides glimpses into what "this 'civilization'" might be in her last novel, *Between the Acts*.

Exploring Woolf's "keen sensitivity to war," Nancy Topping Bazin and Jane Hamovit Lauter argue that "In *Between the Acts* ... Woolf focuses on the threat war poses to civilization and, in particular, to art. Art is what captures the essence of the individual, the culture, or both, and giving it form renders it 'eternal.'"[61] Poesis, or making, represents the antithesis to war, according to Elaine Scarry, whose *The Body in Pain* analyzes the rhetoric of war.[62] Set in the summer of 1939 but written in 1940–41, *Between the Acts* provides, through the mechanism of what might be called an avant-garde village pageant, a *mise en abyme* of artistic production. Bazin and Lauter focus on the role of Miss La Trobe, the director of the pageant, as an artist who staves off the civilization-destroying effects of war: "Through Miss La Trobe's pursuit of her aesthetic vision, there is a hope for order and harmony. If the artist ceases to work, the essence of pattern, the order and harmony, will not be intuited and preserved."[63]

Jed Esty, reading from a cultural studies perspective, sees Miss La Trobe's pageant as a sign of Woolf's turn from modernist, cosmopolitan, "metropolitan vision" in her work to a revaluation of Englishness as an "Island culture" whose national traditions might offer a sense of communal vision able to restore civilization on a local, rather than international or imperial, level:

> The reorientation of anthropological thinking to problems of national self-representation provided the method for English intellectuals to channel the potential energy of a contracting British civilization into a resurgent discourse of national particularism. Virginia Woolf and T. S. Eliot, two writers with apparently divergent ideological profiles and a common position at the institutional center of English modernism, both participated in an anthropological turn that sharpened the autocritical aspects of their own modernist practice. Attuned to the failure of interwar cosmopolitanism and to art's increasing social marginality, Eliot and Woolf turned their attention to the possibilities embodied in shared national traditions and public rituals.[64]

Woolf's presumed turn to "shared national traditions and public rituals" may not be an admission of failure, however, and her eloquent plea in the midst of World War II bombings, to "think peace into existence" and to "give [the young fighting man] access to the creative feelings," would suggest that she was not willing to concede to "art's increasing social marginality."[65]

If poesis, making, "the creative feelings," are a bulwark against destructive aggressive impulses, "the desire to dominate and enslave," then Woolf's nesting of a history within a play within a novel – effectively situating the reader in the position of the audience of the play (as well as of the book) – provides an invitation to read that history, and that play, reparatively.[66] As Sedgwick suggests, "the reparatively positioned reader tries to organize the fragments and part-objects she encounters or creates." Miss La Trobe's pageant dissolves into "fragments and part-objects" as soon as the play's chronology reaches recent English history (i.e., the early twentieth century, or "the present time"):

> Out they leapt, jerked, skipped. Flashing, dazzling, dancing, jumping. Now old Bart ... he was caught. Now Manresa. Here a nose ... There a skirt ... Then trousers only ... Now perhaps a face ... Ourselves? But that's cruel. To snap us as we are, before we've had time to assume ... And only, too, in parts ... That's what's so distorting and upsetting and utterly unfair. Mopping, mowing, whisking, frisking, the looking glasses darted, flashed, exposed. People in the back rows stood up to see the fun. Down they sat, caught themselves ... What an awful show-up! Even for the old who, one might suppose, hadn't any longer any care about their faces ... And Lord! the jangle and the din! The very cows joined in. Walloping, tail lashing, the reticence of nature was undone, and the barriers which should divide Man the Master from the Brute were dissolved. (BTA 184)

These fragments and "part-objects" are disconcerting to the audience on both a sensory level and an ideological one, for the veneer of civilization that "divide[s] Man the Master from the Brute" has crumbled. The natural world – cows, swallows, rain, and so forth – plays a part in this history, throwing into dispute the unquestioned status of "man" as the prime actor, the rational actor in the procession of history.

This upheaval, not surprisingly, brings more questions to the audience's mind than answers. After Reverend Streatfield's response to the play spectacularly fails at delivering a coherent summation, the audience members are left to grapple for meaning in the wake of events: "He said she meant we all act. Yes, but whose play? Ah, that's the question! And if we're left asking questions, isn't it a failure, as a play? I must say I like to feel sure if I go to the theatre, that I've grasped the meaning" (BTA 199–200). Despite the audience's confusion, the phrase "we all act" echoes Leonard Woolf's understanding of civilization as a process bound up with "communal action."[67] Thus, while the chaotic, mirroring action in the foreground dazzles and distracts the audience, actors are shown "rebuilding" civilization in the background of the concluding scene – "Mr. Page the reporter, licking his pencil, noted: 'With the very limited means at her disposal, Miss La Trobe conveyed to the audience Civilization (the wall) in ruins; rebuilt (witness man with hod) by human effort; witness also woman handing bricks. Any fool could grasp that'" (BTA 181).

Woolf, like the playwright Miss LaTrobe, leaves her audience on the precipice of knowing in *Between the Acts*. She does so literally, for she took her own life before the novel was published and we therefore don't know how the story would have ended had she gone back to it one more time.[68] And she does so within the workings of the novel, setting up a series of nested or networked possible new beginnings within the closing scenes. Miss LaTrobe, for example, is already contemplating her next play as she packs up and exits the site of the pageant:

> It was growing dark. Since there were no clouds to trouble the sky, the blue was bluer, the green greener. There was no longer a view – no Folly, no spire of Bolney Minster. It was land merely, no land in particular. She put down her case and stood looking at the land. Then something rose to the surface. "I should group them," she murmured, "here." It would be midnight; there would be two figures, half concealed by a rock. The curtain would rise. What would the first words be? The words escaped her.

Lucy Swithin has returned in a haphazard way to the "Outline of History," projecting her imagined image of "prehistoric man" onto her waking brother, a retired military officer. "'Prehistoric man,' she read, 'half-human, half-ape, roused himself from his semi-crouching and raised great stones'" (BTA 218). Giles and Isa retreat to the bedroom to process the day's personal treacheries – "Alone, enmity was bared; also love. Before they slept, they must fight; after they fought, they would embrace. From that embrace another life might be born. But first they must fight as the dog fox fights with the vixen, in the heart of darkness, in the fields of night" (BTA 219). Woolf's allusion to *Heart of Darkness* in this scene is not coincidental. A life may be produced, but the context of its potential making is rife with images of savagery – not, or not merely, of the bestial kind, but of the human, "civilized" kind that Conrad exposed so brutally in his depiction of Belgian colonialism. One could read this as a foreshadowing of barbarous reproduction – of class, caste, race, social power – but this is not the last scene or the last word in the novel. The last scene – "then the curtain rose. They spoke" – belongs to unspecified actors who begin the dialogue as the book closes.

The next conversation, Woolf seems to be saying, belongs to us.

# Epilogue
# Woolf's Legacy

Virginia Woolf drowned herself in the River Ouse on March 28, 1941. Her suicide has become one of the most-known things about her life, due in part to the lyrical and haunting representation of that event in Stephen Daldry's 2002 Hollywood film, *The Hours*. While it is impossible to know exactly what was going through Woolf's mind on that Friday in March, many have nevertheless speculated on her psychological state. Some, such as the wife of the Bishop of Lincoln, presumed to know Woolf's mind and to find it wanting. According to Hermione Lee, the Bishop's wife wrote "an outraged letter to the Sunday Times" castigating the coroner at Woolf's inquest for apparently showing compassion with his suggestion that Woolf felt "the general beastliness of things more than most people."[1] As both Lee and archivist Sybil Oldfield point out, the Bishop's wife's nasty public letter got the facts of the case wrong, in part due to the coroner's misquotation of Woolf's suicide note to Leonard Woolf. The accurate text of Woolf's letter makes it clear that Woolf was worried about the onset of another mental breakdown (potentially a severe manic episode) that would encumber her loved ones (Leonard and Vanessa) should the Nazis succeed in their threatened invasion. This worry was not the paranoid fantasy of someone in the grip of unreason: the Germans were pounding Britain with heavy air strikes in March of 1941, and Sussex, where the Woolfs lived, is close to the English Channel. Lee, commenting on a draft of Woolf's suicide note, argues, "this generous, careful, precise letter ... is not the letter of an irrational or mad person, but of a person ... suffering from a terrible fear of the possibility of a breakdown with no recovery. The writing of the letter, and the act it presaged, though an act *in extremis*, was rational, deliberate, and courageous."[2]

olf's death was made public, Leonard Woolf received
̣ᴗ̣ɪence letters from friends, neighbors, business acquain-
, and the general public. As Oldfield notes, Woolf's death
ɔccurred during an extremely difficult time for the British, as Nazi
Germany and its allies controlled much of continental Europe, and the
United States had yet to enter the war as allies to the British.[3] That
members of the reading public in Britain were moved to send letters
during such a trying time is a testament to Woolf's impact on ordinary
"common readers." One writer, M. Agnes Smith, a textile weaver who
corresponded with Virginia Woolf about *Three Guineas*, wrote:

> I only knew Mrs. Woolf through her books, and latterly, her letters to me: but
> I felt her books revealed the woman and I loved her ... She gave much which
> has been of value to the world, and what she gave will endure. I feel that
> strongly, despite the chaotic state of things at the present.[4]

Seventy-five years after Smith's letter was posted, Woolf still gives
"much ... of value to the world." Of primary significance was her
insistence that words matter, not just for what they say to us, but for
what they do to us and through us.

## CRAFTSWOMANSHIP

In her 1916 *Times Literary Supplement* essay "Hours in a Library,"
Woolf distinguishes the "man who loves learning" from the "man
who loves reading," depicting the former as a "sedentary, concen-
trated solitary enthusiast, who searches through books to discover
some particular grain of truth upon which he has set his heart."[5]
Conversely, the "man who loves reading" is sociable and "essentially
young" –

> He is a man of intense curiosity; of ideas; open minded and communicative,
> to whom reading is more of the nature of brisk exercise in the open air than of
> sheltered study; he trudges the high road, he climbs higher and higher upon
> the hills until the atmosphere is almost too fine to breathe in; to him it is not
> a sedentary pursuit at all.[6]

For Woolf, then, the trajectory of reading is outward, connecting the
self to the world. One might call such "brisk" activity a form of

askesis, only the practice is imagined as self-nurturing and self-fashioning, rather than self-disciplining and self-denying. Reading as askesis brings us into contact with the world and prepares us to enjoy that contact. Reading is valuable for what its active performance does to us (exercising our minds and emotions) more than for the inert things – concepts, information – it conveys to us to store away in our minds.

Developing a penchant for stimulating that active performance, Woolf adopts a stance of epistemic humility in her critical work – her many essays for the *Times Literary Supplement*, her Hogarth pamphlet essays, newspaper and magazine articles, and her BBC radio broadcasts. Disavowing her expertise, she concludes "Hours in a Library" with the disclaimer "Far be it from us to hazard any theory of art," but then speculates further, "It may be that we shall never know more about it than we know by nature, and our longer experience of it teaches us this only – that of all our pleasures those we get from the great artists are indisputably among the best; and more we may not know."[7] Woolf's humility – part rhetorical device, part genuine admission of the limits of knowledge, and part invitation to engage – is characteristic of much of Woolf's critical practice throughout her career. The structure of her thought is apophatic – meaning that she begins with a denial, something along the lines of "I can't possibly give you an answer to this unanswerable question" – and then proceeds to offer a speculative answer to the unanswerable question. Hence, after she humbly denies being able to "hazard any theory of art," she nevertheless offers a theory of what literary art does to us:

> But, advancing no theory, we shall find one or two qualities in such works as these which we can hardly expect to find in books made within the span of our lifetime ... But all our faculties are summoned to the task, as in the great moments of our own experience; and some consecration descends upon us from their hands which we return to life, feeling it more keenly and understanding it more deeply than before.[8]

As a "public intellectual," someone who engaged prolifically with the reading public on matters of great import (contributing to "knowledge which determines communal action ... social behavior, or the general economic conditions of a community," in the words of Leonard Woolf), Woolf's aesthetic practice aligns with her critical standards.[9]

That is, her novels connect her readers to the world of ideas in a way that "return[s them] to life, feeling it more keenly and understanding it more deeply than before."[10] An anonymous "common reader," immigrated to England presumably due to the hardships of World War II, perhaps expressed this best in a condolence letter to Leonard Woolf:

> I have to use a language which I have not yet mastered ... but as far as words can penetrate darkness and silence let me tell you that there are many who feel like you the great loss ... I have read several books by Virginia Woolf and just now am reading Roger Fry's life. Her high belief in Art, the belief in the mission of the artist, made me esteem her so highly. And whatever as a foreigner I learned of English I thank to her. The beauty and subtleness of her language simply struck me ... Artists must know that they are understood and that there are "Common Readers" in the background. We would have needed her courage and honesty for the struggle ahead against the philistines in every field.[11]

Near the end of her life, in a 1937 radio broadcast for the BBC, Woolf attributes this aesthetic power to words themselves. She begins her talk with her typical apophatic gesture, first noting that "the title of this series is 'Words Fail Me,'" and then suggesting that her title, "Craftsmanship," can't do what it promises – "there is something incongruous, unfitting, about the term 'craftsmanship' when applied to words."[12] Words cannot be subjected to the control of the craftsperson, she suggests, because words are living and unpredictable things, resistant to artifice that would pin them down. Words are instead more pliable to those who would cajole and coax them to generate, perhaps even "procreate in a beautiful medium" in keeping with Diotima's concept of love:

> Thus one sentence of the simplest kind rouses the imagination, the memory, the eye and the ear – all combine in reading it. But they combine – they combine unconsciously together. The moment we single out and emphasize the suggestions as we have done here they become unreal; and we, too, become unreal – specialists, word mongers, phrase finders, not readers. In reading we have to allow the sunken meanings to remain sunken, suggested, not stated; lapsing and flowing into each other like reeds on the bed of a river.[13]

Not exactly passive, reading nevertheless involves giving up some control over meanings and admitting that language is culturally formed and transformed. To paraphrase philosopher Ludwig Wittgenstein, it does not make sense to think of language as strictly private (i.e., as intelligible to only one person).[14] Therefore, reading is a communal practice that reaches beyond ourselves, even when done in solitude.

Woolf thus emphasizes the social and accumulative nature of language as a gift as well as a challenge to the writer:

> Everyone who has every written a sentence knows that words, English words, are fully of echoes, of memories, of associations – naturally. They have been out and about, on people's lips, in their houses, in the streets and in the fields, for so many centuries. And that is one of the chief difficulties in writing them today – that they are so stored with meanings, with memories, that they have contracted so many famous marriages.[15]

It is comforting to know that language was not dead, but proliferating (propagating, if we take the metaphor of "marriages" seriously), for Woolf in 1937 when she was composing *Three Guineas*, her scathing indictment of patriarchal education and its links to fascist sentiments, aggression, and war.

Words are not necessarily dead in times of trouble (perhaps they do not fail Woolf after all?) but they grow moribund through complacency. In her earlier (1932) "Letter to a Young Poet," Woolf comforts a hypothetical young poet who is despairing over the seeming "death" of poetry in his contemporary era (a familiar stance that poets such as Matthew Arnold adopted when comparing their era to previous eras). In her letter, she argues that poetic language is not dying, but, rather, going through a phase of awkward recalcitrance because modern poets are trying out new styles and subjects for expression:

> Still, consider the symptoms. They are not the symptoms of death in the least. Death in literature, and I need not tell you how often literature has died in this country or in that, comes gracefully, smoothly, quietly. Lines slip easily down the accustomed grooves. The old designs are copied so glibly that we are half inclined to think them original, save for that very glibness. But here the very opposite is happening: here in my first quotation the poet breaks his machine because he will clog it with raw fact. In my second, he is unintelligible because of his desperate determination to tell the truth about himself. Thus I cannot help thinking that though you may be right in talking of the difficulty of the time, you are wrong to despair.[16]

Woolf's admonition not to despair as long as language is unruly and recalcitrant calls to mind the public intellectual work of a contemporary writer who, perhaps not coincidentally, wrote about Virginia Woolf in her Master's thesis: Toni Morrison, who received the Nobel Prize for Literature in 1993.

Much like Woolf, who used storytelling to get her message across (via the fictional frame of her narrator's rambles through "Oxbridge" in *A Room of One's Own*, or the epistolary framework which channels the rhetorical fire of *Three Guineas*), Morrison uses storytelling to comment on social issues and ethical concerns. Thus, Morrison presents a parable in her Nobel Prize acceptance speech. Morrison's story offers two perspectives (the perspective of age and wisdom and the perspective of youth and curiosity) in her parable of the community's responsibility for a fragile "bird in the hand." The story begins when a group of seemingly rash youths confront an elderly blind woman and ask her to tell them whether the bird they hold in one of their hands is dead or alive. The wise woman turns the tables on the young pranksters by placing the ethical burden of responsibility for the bird onto those who hold it: "I don't know whether the bird you are holding is dead or alive," she retorts, "but what I do know is that it is in your hands."[17] Morrison goes on to explain that in her version of the parable, "I choose to read the bird as language and the woman as a practiced writer. She is worried about how the language she dreams in, given to her at birth, is handled, put into service, even withheld from her for certain nefarious purposes."[18] Language, for Morrison, is "a living thing over which one has control, but mostly as agency – as an act with consequences."[19] Dead language, for Morrison, "is unyielding language content to admire its own paralysis."[20] This "paralysis" is akin to Woolf's own concern for literature that finds itself in a rut, so tightly channeled that death comes to it "gracefully, smoothly, quietly." The lesson of both Woolf's "Letter to a Young Poet" and Morrison's "Nobel Lecture" is that language is alive, unpredictable, in need of careful tending, and powerful. Working with language so that it thrives is a community responsibility, one that, in turn, keeps the community flourishing.

## CULTIVATING THE COMMONS

Woolf's legacy, like the living language that Morrison has inherited and redeployed with responsibility and agency "as an act with consequences," can best be measured by how readers and writers take her up in the present day. That is, Woolf's value is not intrinsic to the things she wrote, although those cultural artifacts are often exquisitely crafted, brave, witty, prescient, and wise. To return to Barbara Herrnstein Smith's insights on the "contingency of value," Woolf's value is part of a complex dynamic relationship between her work and her readers. Woolf has not always been regarded as an invaluable (i.e., "canonical") author in British or even modernist literature. In my lifetime (which is just shy of fifty years, as of this writing), critical regard for Woolf's work at the level of the school or university has gone from *not important* (we were not taught a snippet of Woolf in my North American public high school, despite the excellent reputation of the school's English department) to *experimental* (we read *To the Lighthouse* in my 1984 British literature survey, but were told that to include it on a syllabus where James Joyce or D. H. Lawrence generally resided was a new and even transgressive act) to *expected* reading by the 1990s when I was in graduate school, to *essential* reading for my contemporary students of British literature and modernism. Woolf's works did not change over that timespan, although substantial portions of her diaries and letters were published between 1977 and 1984, offering readers new insights into her life, thoughts, and habits.

While the words of her texts have not changed, the culture and context in which Woolf's writing is read and regarded has changed significantly in the thirty-five years since I started high school. Literary work survives, according to Smith, because it *does* something necessary for its culture: "An object or artifact that performs certain desired/able functions particularly well at a given time for some community of subjects, being perhaps not only 'fit' but exemplary – that is, 'the best of its kind' – under those conditions, will have an immediate survival advantage."[21] In the years immediately after her death, Woolf's words were taken up by a generation or two of readers who grew up in the shadow of the barbarity of World War II and the Holocaust; the subsequent anticolonial movements in South Asia and Africa; and the Civil Rights, Feminist, Gay Liberation, and Anti-War movements of the late 1960s and 1970s. Woolf's anti-imperial, feminist, pacifist, and antihomophobic sentiments drew new readers to her work as these movements permeated North American and Western European cultures. The beauty of her prose, its stylistic virtuosity, its wicked wit and philosophical acuity keeps readers of subsequent generations coming back for more. As Smith explains, "canonical work begins not merely to *survive within*, but to *shape* and *create* the culture in which its value is produced and transmitted and, for that very reason, to perpetuate the conditions of its own flourishing."[22]

This is not to say that Woolf's work was taken up merely for political or social reasons and now persists because it has succeeded in shaping the world in its political image. Smith notes that "works that are structurally complex and, in the technical sense, information-rich – and which, by virtue of those qualities, may be especially amenable to multiple reconfiguration, are more likely to enter into relation with the emergent interests of various subjects, and thus more likely adaptable to emergent conditions."[23] Woolf's oeuvre is nothing if not "structurally complex," from her earliest experiments with narrative perspective in "A Mark on the Wall," to her sparse psychological probing in *Jacob's Room*, to her use of free indirect discourse in *Mrs. Dalloway*, to her idiosyncratic and moving rendering of "Time Passing" in *To the Lighthouse*, to her playful (and meaningful) breaches of biographical form in *Flush* and *Orlando*, to her atom-like structure and extraordinary use of dramatic/interior monologue in *The Waves*, to her rhetorical tour de force in *Three Guineas*, to her adventurous play-poem-pageant novel *Between the Acts*.[24] Woolf's structural complexity is not merely formal, however, and that is why her work still speaks to generations brought up on far more complex digital media than even Woolf could have imagined a century ago. Woolf's style is always evolving, although always built from impeccable, elegant syntax that does not go stale, perhaps because it is always used in service to a new creative "combination" of energetic (live) words.

Moreover, as I have endeavored to show in previous chapters, Woolf's writing addresses persistent philosophical questions that have endured for centuries, not because of their complexity, but because of their simplicity. Such questions are simultaneously unanswerable and yet absolutely crucial for forging a life worth living. How is one to live? What makes for a good life? A free life? What is my responsibility to others? What is love and how ought I practice it? How do I intervene in cultural practices, customs, and institutions that appear brutal, unfair, and unjust if I am only one voice, and a small voice at that? More than anything, Woolf gave the world the gift of her example as an intrepid writer and thinker who took on these questions without embarrassment or unnecessary embellishment. Although she did not receive a university degree, she was nonetheless a philosopher who plied her trade in the *agora* of her time – that is, in the public realm as Hannah Arendt describes it: "To live together in the world means essentially that a world of things is between those who have it in common, as a table is located between those who sit around it ... The public realm, as the common world, gathers us together and yet prevents our falling over each other, so to speak."[25]

The public realm, for Arendt, is the common ground for "action (*praxis*) and speech (*lexis*), out of which rises the realm of human affairs."[26] Woolf flung her speech into the commons through the newspaper, print periodicals, and literature published by her own press. Operating that small press, not incidentally, constituted an action which helped bring lesser-known voices (of the working class, of women, of young writers and dissident political thinkers) to the commons, as well. She did not disavow her own precarity, yet nevertheless took up the responsibility of "thinking [as her] fighting" despite the incredible odds stacked against her as a woman, a survivor of childhood sexual abuse, a person with a misunderstood (and possibly misdiagnosed) mental illness which she negotiated with grace and courage, and a free thinker and sexual outlaw in an era when nonnormativity was policed with vitriol.[27]

For these reasons Woolf's legacy exceeds her written work. If it persists, as I believe it will, it will be because she lived the life of a thinker who was not afraid to inquire into the meaning of life, and yet was very wary of telling others how to live their lives. Arguing for "intellectual liberty" from an engaged standpoint – that is, not from a quietist position outside the agora, but from an "outsider's" standpoint from within its metaphorical boundaries – Woolf claims, "There we have in embryo the creature, Dictator as we call him when he is Italian or German, who believes that he has the right, whether given by God, Nature, sex or race is immaterial, to dictate to other human beings how they shall live; what they shall do" (TG 65). Like Socrates, for whom the questions of how to live and what to do were so significant that he was willing to brave the displeasure of Athenian leaders in order to keep asking his questions in public, without shame, Woolf left her readers with more than a record of her works. She left us the example of her practice.

# Notes

## INTRODUCTION ON VALUE

1. Barbara Herrnstein Smith, *Contingencies of Value: Alternative Perspectives for Critical Theory* (Cambridge: Harvard University Press, 1988), 127.
2. Ibid.
3. Ibid., 30.
4. Consensus may of course be influenced by power. That is, in a class-stratified society, the ruling class may hold sway over what is considered valuable in a community through inordinate influence over the means of production of artistic projects and of the dissemination of information/education about what is deemed valuable in the culture. Smith does not dispute the role of ideology in forging communal agreement. Rather, class stratification, power, educational authority, control of the means of production and dissemination of cultural artifacts would all be part of the many contingencies that go into determining aesthetic value.
5. Smith, *Contingencies of Value*, 40; italics in original.
6. Ibid., 32.
7. Melba Cuddy-Keane, *Virginia Woolf, the Intellectual, and the Public Sphere* (New York: Cambridge University Press, 2003), 177; italics in original.
8. Jean-Michel Rabaté writes in his 2013 Introduction to *A Handbook of Modernism Studies*, "We can also remember that, not so long ago, such an influential critic as Hugh Kenner refused to grant the epithet of 'modernist' to Virginia Woolf, who was deemed too 'soft' and not experimental enough, reserving the term to the group animated by Ezra Pound, a group including, it is true, Hilda Doolittle alias H. D. And Gertrude Stein could state that all geniuses were men – which included her as well!" Jean-Michel Rabaté, *A Handbook of Modernism Studies* (Hoboken: Wiley, 2013), 4.

9. John Guillory, *Cultural Capital: The Problem of Literary Canon Formation*, Kindle edn. (Chicago: University of Chicago Press, 2013), ix.

10. Raymond Williams, "Culture is Ordinary," in *Conviction* (London: Macgibbon & Key, 1958), 93.

11. Ibid.

12. Adrienne Rich, "Claiming an Education (1977)," in *On Lies, Secrets, and Silence: Selected Prose 1966–1978* (New York: W. W. Norton, 1979), 231.

13. Virginia Woolf, *Three Guineas* (1938), annotated and introduced by Jane Marcus (New York: Harcourt Inc., 2006), 33. Further citations of *Three Guineas* will appear parenthetically in the text, abbreviated *TG*.

14. I take the term "conviviality" from Paul Gilroy's *Postcolonial Melancholia* (New York: Columbia University Press, 2005), xv.

15. Cuddy-Keane, *Virginia Woolf, the Intellectual, and the Public Sphere*, 22.

16. Q. D. Leavis, *Fiction and the Reading Public* (London: Chatto & Windus, 1939). Reprinted in Kindle edition by Read Books Ltd. (2013), 5.

17. Ibid., 7.

18. Patrick Wintour, "Facebook and Bebo Risk 'Infantilising' the Human Mind." *The Guardian*, February 24, 2009. www.theguardian.com/uk/2009/feb/24/social-networking-site-changing-childrens-brains.

19. William Wordsworth, "Preface to *Lyrical Ballads*," (1802), in *The Norton Anthology of English Literature*, 7th edn., vol. 2A, ed. M. H. Abrams and Jack Stillinger (New York: W. W. Norton, 2000), 243. Matthew Arnold, "The Function of Criticism at the Present Time," in *The Norton Anthology of English Literature*, 7th edn., vol. 2B, ed. Carol T. Christ (New York: W. W. Norton, 2000), 1525.

20. Pew Research Center, "Younger Americans and Public Libraries," September 10, 2014, www.pewinternet.org/2014/09/10/younger-americans-and-public-libraries/ Accessed September 16, 2015.

21. Cuddy-Keane examines Woolf's concern with access to education for working class men and women in *Virginia Woolf, The Intellectual and the Public Sphere*, and specifically notes Woolf's appreciation for the public or "free" library as "alternative pedagogy," 109–10.

22. Virginia Woolf, "Middlebrow" in *The Death of the Moth and Other Essays*, ed. Leonard Woolf (New York: Harcourt Brace and Company, 1970), 183–84.

23. Ibid., 183; emphasis in original.
24. Virginia Woolf, "How Should One Read a Book?" in *The Second Common Reader*, ed. Andrew McNeillie (New York: Harcourt Brace Jovanovich, 1986), 258.
25. Virginia Woolf, *Between the Acts* (New York: Harcourt Brace Jovanovich, 1969), 181. Hereafter referenced as BTA.
26. Virginia Woolf, "Thoughts on Peace in an Air Raid," in *The Death of the Moth and Other Essays*, ed. Leonard Woolf (New York: Harcourt Brace & Company, 1970), 248; Audre Lorde, "The Master's Tools will Never Dismantle the Master's House," *Sister Outsider* (Freedom: The Crossing Press, 1984), 110–13.
27. Woolf, "Thoughts on Peace," 247–48.
28. Virginia Woolf, "Craftsmanship," in *The Death of the Moth and Other Essays*, ed. Leonard Woolf (New York: Harcourt, Brace & Company, 1970), 203–05.
29. Ibid., 206.
30. Virginia Woolf, *A Room of One's Own* [1929] (New York: Harcourt Brace & Company, 1981), 41.
31. Because it is more familiar to readers, I use the term "mental illness" throughout this book to indicate Woolf's cognitive/affective atypicality (probably bipolar disorder). My own inclination would be to use the less wieldy term "cognitive/affective atypicality" to indicate Woolf's condition. For more on my reasoning, see "Woolf and Crip Theory," in *Blackwell Companion to Virginia Woolf*, ed. Jessica Berman (New York: Wiley-Blackwell, in press). There are far too many excellent works on Woolf for me to list them all here, so let me first indicate my indebtedness to Woolf scholars in general and the scholarship of those in the International Virginia Woolf Society for their careful and comprehensive work on the contexts of Woolf's life, thought, and writing. For a recent, extensive collection of work contextualizing Woolf, see Bryony Randall and Jane Goldman, eds., *Virginia Woolf in Context* (New York: Cambridge University Press, 2012). With apologies to those I may have missed, listed below are some, among the many, significant scholarly works on Woolf: Jane Marcus, *Virginia Woolf and the Languages of Patriarchy* (Bloomington, Indiana University Press, 1987); Mark Hussey, ed., *Virginia Woolf and War: Fiction, Reality, and Myth* (Syracuse: Syracuse University Press, 1991); Brenda Silver, *Virginia Woolf Icon* (Chicago: The University of Chicago Press, 1999); Alex Zwerdling, *Virginia Woolf and the Real World* (Berkeley: University of California Press, 1986); Christine Froula, *Virginia Woolf and the Bloomsbury*

*Avant-Garde: War, Civilization, Modernity* (New York: Columbia University Press, 2005); Hermione Lee, *Virginia Woolf* (New York: Random House, 1996); Louise Desalvo, *Virginia Woolf: The Impact of Childhood Sexual Abuse on Her Life and Work* (New York: Beacon Press, 1989); Melba Cuddy-Keane, *Virginia Woolf, the Intellectual, and the Public Sphere*; Ann Banfield, The *Phantom Table: Woolf, Fry, Russell and the Epistemology of Modernism* (New York: Cambridge: 2000); Anne Fernald, *Virginia Woolf, Feminism, and the Reader* (New York: Palgrave MacMillan, 2006), Pamela L. Caughie, *Virginia Woolf and Postmodernism: Literature in Quest and Question of Itself* (Urbana: University of Illinois Press, 1991), and Bonnie Kime Scott, *In the Hollow of the Wave: Virginia Woolf and Modernist Uses of Nature* (Charlottesville: University of Virginia Press, 2012).

## I  EUDEMONIA: THE NECESSARY ART OF LIVING

1. *The Hours*, dir. Stephen Daldry, screenplay by David Hare, and novel by Michael Cunningham (Scott Rudin/Rupert Fox Production, 2002).
2. See, for example, Thomas Caramagno, *The Flight of the Mind: Virginia Woolf's Art and Manic-Depressive Illness* (Berkeley: University of California Press, 1992); Louise Desalvo, *Impact of Childhood Sexual Abuse*; and Suzette Henke and David Eberly, eds., *Virginia Woolf and Trauma: Embodied Texts* (New York: Pace University Press, 2007).
3. Kirsty Martin, "Virginia Woolf's Happiness," *Essays in Criticism* 64, no. 4 (2014): 398. Martin argues (rightly, I believe) that happiness is far more important to Woolf's *oeuvre* than previous critics have made it out to be, and through a careful reading of *Mrs. Dalloway* links the concept to Woolf's concern with privacy and post–World War I national interest in the mental health of the British population.
4. Aristotle, *Nicomachean Ethics*, trans. W. D. Ross, in *Introduction to Aristotle*, ed. Richard McKeon (New York: Modern Library College Editions, 1947), 1.7.
5. Sara Ahmed, *The Promise of Happiness* (Durham: Duke University Press, 2010), 50, 88, 121.
6. Patricia Curd, "Aristotelian Visions of Moral Character," *Feminism and Ancient Philosophy*, ed. Julie K. Ward (New York: Routledge, 1996): 142. Jim Stewart also discusses the influence of Aristotle's *Poetics* on Woolf's early career as a reviewer in "'Poetics ... will fit me for a reviewer!' Aristotle and Woolf's

Journalism," in *Virginia Woolf in Context*, ed. Bryony Randall and Jane Goldman (New York: Cambridge University Press, 2012): 322–31.

7. The finding aid for the Leonard and Virginia Woolf Library at Washington State University includes three volumes that include Aristotle's *Ethics*, among them volumes 1, 7, 9, and 11 of *The Works of Aristotle Translated into English*, ed. W. D. Ross (Oxford: Clarendon Press, 1908–52). Volume 9, first published in 1915, contains the *Nicomachean Ethics*. Julia King and Laila Miletic-Vejzovic, eds., *The Library of Leonard and Virginia Woolf: A Short-title Catalogue* (Pullman: Washington State University Press, 2003), http://ntserver1 .wsulibs.wsu.edu/masc/onlinebooks/woolflibrary/woolflibraryon line.htm. Leonard Woolf read Aristotle's *Ethics* in 1902, according to his July 28 letter to Lytton Strachey. *Letters of Leonard Woolf*, ed. Frederic Spotts (New York: Harcourt Brace Jovanovich, 1989), 25.

8. Koulouris offers a thorough and thoughtful study of what he calls Woolf's "greekness," a somewhat subversive feminist strain of the Hellenism, which, in its less subversive strain, he associates with male academic study of Greek. It is clear from Woolf's "Greek Notebook," which Koulouris analyzes comprehensively, that Woolf read Plato and Sophocles, as well as Homer in the Greek, and would have been familiar with Ancient Greek philosophy from her own reading as well as from the influence of her tutors, Janet Case and Clara Pater, or her male Bloomsbury compatriots. See Theodore Koulouris, *Hellenism and Loss in the Work of Virginia Woolf* (Burlington: Ashgate, 2011).

9. Aristotle, *Nicomachean Ethics* I, 13.

10. Woolf, "Thoughts on Peace," 247–48. My thanks to philosopher Gaile Pohlhaus, Jr. for helping me to think through the *Nicomachean Ethics* and for suggesting the term "virtuosity" as a way to conceive of virtue and excellence woven together.

11. Richard Parry, "Ancient Ethical Theory," in *The Stanford Encyclopedia of Philosophy*, ed. Edward N. Zalta, Fall 2014 edition, http://plato.stanford.edu/archives/fall2014/entries/ethics-ancient/.

12. Woolf, "How Should One Read a Book?" 258.

13. Virginia Woolf, *The Diary of Virginia Woolf Vol. 3 (1925–1930)*, ed. Anne Olivier Bell and Andrew McNeillie (New York: Harcourt Brace Jovanovich, 1980), April 29, 1930.

14. Woolf, *Diary*, May 1, 1930, qtd. in Perry Meisel, *The Absent Father: Virginia Woolf and Walter Pater* (New Haven: Yale University Press, 1980), 78.

15. Meisel, *The Absent Father*, 78.
16. Meisel, *The Absent Father*, 73–90.
17. Walter Pater, "Conclusion to *The Renaissance: Studies in Art and Poetry*," in *Selected Writings of Walter Pater*, ed. Harold Bloom (New York: Columbia, 1974), 59.
18. Elaine Scarry juxtaposes the creative process of making with the destructive process of war in *The Body in Pain: The Making and Unmaking of the World* (New York: Oxford University Press, 1985), 161. I return to this concept in Chapter 4.
19. Rebecca Goldstein, *Plato at the Googleplex: Why Philosophy Won't Go Away* (New York: Pantheon Books, 2014), 129.
20. Virginia Woolf, *The Waves*, annotated and with an introduction by Molly Hite (New York: Harcourt Inc., 2006), 220; further references to this edition are cited parenthetically in the text as (W).
21. Noel Annan, *Leslie Stephen: The Godless Victorian* (Chicago: The University of Chicago Press, 1984), 45–47; Leslie Stephen, *An Agnostic's Apology and Other Essays*, 2nd edn. (New York: G. P. Putnam's Sons, 1903).
22. Animal studies scholars would argue as well that subsuming non-human life into a means for human ends (sustenance through eating animals or labor by using horses, dogs, dolphins, elephants, etc., for work) is unethical. I confine my argument here to human instrumentalization, but it is not necessarily limited to human animals.
23. Virginia Woolf, *Jacob's Room* (New York: Harcourt Brace Jovanovich, 1950), 79; hereafter noted in parenthetical citations as (JR).
24. Thomas Beattie, "Moments of Meaning Dearly Achieved: Virginia Woolf's Sense of an Ending," *MFS Modern Fiction Studies* 32, no. 4 (1986): 522.
25. "Reader, I married him" is from Charlotte Brontë, *Jane Eyre* (New York: Bantam Books, 1987), 429. On Woolf's twist on the bildungsroman, see Christine Froula, "Out of the Chrysalis: Female Initiation and Female Authority in Virginia Woolf's *The Voyage Out*," *Tulsa Studies in Women's Literature* 5, no. 1 (Spring, 1986): 63–90; and Susan Stanford Friedman, "Spatialization, Narrative Theory, and Virginia Woolf's *The Voyage Out*," in *Ambiguous Discourse: Feminist Narratology and British Women Writers*, ed. Kathy Mezei (Chapel Hill: University of North Carolina Press, 1996): 122–36.
26. Herbert Marcuse, "The Ideology of Death," in *The Meaning of Death*, ed. Herman Feifel (New York: McGraw Hill, 1959), 65.

27. Ibid., 65.
28. Even Mrs. Thornbury lets down her guard as the upholder of Victorian propriety and rejects her public display of consoling rationalization when she is alone in private: "When she was alone by herself she clenched her fists together, and began beating the back of a chair with them. She was like a wounded animal. She hated death; she was furious, outraged, indignant with death, as if it were a living creature. She refused to relinquish her friends to death. She would not submit to the dark and nothingness" (359).

## 2  INCANDESCENCE: ATTENTION AND ILLUMINATION

1. Iris Murdoch, *The Sovereignty of Good* (New York: Routledge, 2001), 17. Italics in original.
2. Thomas Nagel, *The View from Nowhere* (New York: Oxford University Press, 1986), 70.
3. Meisel, *The Absent Father*, 98.
4. José Medina develops the concept of "epistemic insensitivity" in *The Epistemology of Resistance: Gender and Racial Oppression, Epistemic Injustice, and the Social Imagination* (New York: Oxford University Press, 2013), xii.
5. Donna Haraway, "Situated Knowledges: The Science Question in Feminism and the Privilege of Partial Perspective," *Feminist Studies* 14, no. 3 (Autumn, 1988): 589.
6. Ibid.
7. The term "disinterested" is not of necessity aligned with a defense of the status quo. Cuddy-Keane notes in her discussion of the Worker's Educational Association that working-class advocates and activists called for more disinterestedness among educators in universities. According to Cuddy-Keane, the 1909 report of the "Joint Committee of University and Working-class Representatives on the Relation of the University to the Higher Education of Workpeople" found university culture "too removed from general life, and *not sufficiently disinterested*" to "prepare workers to be effective members of society in a self-governing nation." Cuddy-Keane, *Virginia Woolf, the Intellectual, and the Public Sphere*, 87 (emphasis in original).
8. *The OED*, for example, defines incandescent as "Emitting light on account of being a high temperature, glowing with heat ... Glowing, brightly shining, brilliantly luminous" and "Becoming or being warm

or intense in feeling, expression, etc.; ardent, fiery; 'flaming up.'" *Oxford English Dictionary*, 2nd edn., vol. 7, prepared by J. A. Simpson and E. S. C. Weiner (New York: Oxford University Press, 1989), 781.

9. I am indebted to the poet Cathy Wagner for her reminder that incandescent light bulbs are not only glowing, but connected to sources of power.

10. See, for example, Charlie Scott, "Get Out of Your Own Head: Mindful Listening for Project Managers," *SANS Institute InfoSec Reading Room*, December 19, 2010, www.sans.org/reading-room/whitepa pers/leadership/head-mindful-listening-project-managers-33563, accessed September 22, 2015; or Ginger Kern, "8 Healthy Ways to Get Out of Your Own Head," The Feel Good Lifestyle, August 22, 1012, www.thefeelgoodlifestyle.com/8-healthy-ways-to-get-out-of-your-h ead.html. Accessed September 22, 2015.

11. Murdoch, *The Sovereignty of Good*, 17. Donna J. Lazenby examines the convergences among Woolf's aesthetic practices and theories and Murdoch's theories and practices in *A Mystical Philosophy: Transcendence and Immanence in the Works of Virginia Woolf and Iris Murdoch* (London: Bloomsbury Publishing, 2014). Lazenby's interesting study focuses on what she sees as both writers' atheist mysticism. While my own interest is in the confluence of Murdoch's and Woolf's moral vision, Lazenby's suggestion that there are synergies between the two thinkers is illuminating.

12. Murdoch, 33.

13. The full scenario reads thus: "A mother, whom I shall call M, feels hostility to her daughter-in-law, whom I shall call D. M finds D quite a good-hearted girl, but while not exactly common yet certainly unpolished and lacking in dignity and refinement. D is inclined to be pert and familiar, insufficiently ceremonious, brusque, sometimes positively rude, always tiresomely juvenile. M does not like D's accent or the way D dresses. M feels that her son has married beneath him. Let us assume for purposes of the example that the mother, who is a very 'correct' person, behaves beautifully to the girl throughout, not allowing her real opinion to appear in any way. We might underline this aspect of the example by supposing that the young couple have emigrated or that D is now dead: the point being to ensure that whatever is in question as happening happens entirely in M's mind." Murdoch, *The Sovereignty of Good*, 16–17.

14. Ibid., 17.

15. Virginia Woolf, *To the Lighthouse*, edited and annotated by Mark Hussey (New York: Harcourt, Inc., 2005), 211.

16. On the importance of "relational knowing," see Gaile Pohlhaus, Jr., "Relational Knowing and Epistemic Injustice: Toward a Theory of Willful Hermeneutical Ignorance," *Hypatia* 27, no. 4 (2012): 715–35.

17. Pater, "Conclusion to *The Renaissance*," 60.

18. Murdoch developed a theory of moral vision as developing a "just and loving gaze." See Maria Antonaccio and William Schweiker, eds., *Iris Murdoch and the Search for Human Goodness* (Chicago: The University of Chicago Press, 1996). See also Nancy Snow, "Iris Murdoch's Notion of a Loving Gaze," *The Journal of Value Inquiry* 39 (2005): 487–98.

19. Medina, *The Epistemology of Resistance*, 28.

20. Ibid., 30.

21. Ibid.

22. Ibid., 31.

23. Ibid., 30–31.

24. Ibid., 33.

25. Ibid., 35.

26. Ibid., 28.

27. Ibid., 43.

28. On the novel's status as a love letter, see Nigel Nicolson, *Portrait of a Marriage: Vita Sackville-West and Harold Nicolson* (Chicago: The University of Chicago Press, 1998), 202; as a queer take on the biography, see Melanie Micir, "The Queer Timing of Orlando: A Biography" *Virginia Woolf Miscellany* 82 (September 2012), 11; as a trans-novel, Chris Coffman, "Woolf's *Orlando* and the Resonances of Trans Studies," *Genders* 51 (2010), https://web.archive.org/web/2013 0512204349/http://www.genders.org/g51/g51_coffman.html. Accessed September 22, 2015.

29. Kari Elise Lokke, "Orlando and Incandescence: Virginia Woolf's Comic Sublime," *Modern Fiction Studies* 38, no. 1 (Spring 1992): 249.

30. According to Horace, "The aim of the poet is either to benefit, or to amuse, or to make his words at once please and give lessons of life." Horace, "The Art of Poetry," in *Horace for English Readers*, trans. E. C. Wickham (London: Oxford University Press, 1930), 357.

31. Virginia Woolf, *Orlando*, annotated and with an introduction by Maria DiBattista (New York: Harcourt, Inc. 2006), hereafter cited as (O).

32. "Genius, n. and adj.," *Oxford English Dictionary*, 2nd edn., vol. 6, prepared by J. A. Simpson and E. S. C. Weiner (New York: Oxford University Press, 1989), 444.

## 3 INTERDEPENDENCE: PATTERN AND PRECARITY

1. Virginia Woolf, *A Sketch of the Past, Moments of Being*, ed. Jeanne Schulkind (New York: Harcourt Brace and Company, 1985), 72.
2. Meisel, *Absent Father*, 176.
3. Julie Kane, "The Varieties of Mystical Experience in the Writings of Virginia Woolf," *Twentieth Century Literature* 41, no. 4: 328–49; Lazenby, *Mystical Philosophy*.
4. Gillian Beer, *Virginia Woolf: The Common Ground* (Ann Arbor: The University of Michigan Press, 1996); Paul Tolliver Brown, "Relativity, Quantum Physics, and Consciousness in Virginia Woolf's *To the Lighthouse*," *Journal of Modern Literature* 32, no. 3 (2009): 39–62; Holly Henry, *Virginia Woolf and the Discourse of Science: The Aesthetics of Astronomy* (New York: Cambridge University Press, 2003).
5. Beer, *Common Ground*, 124.
6. Brown, "Relativity, Quantum Physics, and Consciousness," 40.
7. Henry, *Virginia Woolf and the Discourse of Science*, 109.
8. Ibid.
9. Scholarship on Woolf's perspectives on communalism or radical individual subjectivity is extensive. See, for example, Jeanette McVicker and Laura Davis, eds., *Virginia Woolf and Communities: Selected Papers from the Eighth Annual Conference on Virginia Woolf* (New York: Pace University Press, 1999). As a touchstone of the communalist position, I proffer Melba Cuddy-Keane's "The Politics of Comic Modes in Virginia Woolf's Between the Acts," *PMLA* 105 (1990): 273–85. On the other side of the spectrum, Ann Banfield offers a finely developed exegesis of Woolf's philosophical monadism in *Phantom Table*.
10. Judith Butler, *Precarious Life: The Powers of Mourning and Violence* (New York: Verso, 2004); Dorothy Day, "Poverty and Precarity," *The Catholic Worker* 2, no. 6 (May 1952).
11. Butler, *Precarious Life*, 20.
12. Aldous Huxley, *Brave New World* (New York: Harper Brothers, 1932); Maurice Hurley, "Q Who," *Star Trek: The Next Generation*, 1988.
13. Woolf, *A Sketch of the Past*, 80.
14. Beer, *Common Ground*, 8.
15. Ibid.
16. My thanks to Gaile Pohlhaus, Jr. for pointing out that this question can be attributed to the Oracle at Delphi, whose enjoinder to "know thyself" is interpreted by philosophers such as Pohlhaus as an

injunction to "know your place in relation to the world (cosmos) around you." Email communication, January 30, 2015.

17. Woolf, *A Sketch of the Past*, 80.
18. Ibid., 70.
19. Ibid., 72.
20. John H. Miller and Scott E. Page, *Complex Adaptive Systems: An Introduction to Computational Models of Social Life*, Princeton Studies in Complexity, Kindle edition (Princeton: Princeton University Press, 2007), 7.
21. "The notion that real social systems often result in complex worlds is nothing new. More than two hundred years ago Adam Smith described a world where the self-interested social behavior of butchers, brewers, bakers, and the like resulted in the emergence of a well-defined order," explain Miller and Page, loc. 1074–76. The Leonard and Virginia Woolf Library contains a binder entitled *Adam Smith as Student and Professor*, attributed to Keynes, but more probably a review of William Robert Scott's *Adam Smith as Student and Professor* (Glasgow: Jackson & Son, 1937). The entry in the Woolf Library finding aid reads: "Keynes, John Maynard. *Adam Smith as Student and Professor*. London; New York: Macmillan, 1938. VW – binder." Julia King and Laila Miletic-Vejzovic, eds., *Library of Leonard and Virginia Woolf*.
22. Woolf, *A Sketch of the Past*, 69.
23. Kane, "Varieties of Mystical Experience," 340.
24. Beer, *Common Ground*, 66.
25. Ibid., 71.
26. Ibid.
27. Office of Naval Research, *Science and Technology Focus*, "Ocean in Motion: Waves – Characteristics," Arlington. Accessed January 31, 2015, https://web.archive.org/web/20150205131240/http://www.on r.navy.mil/Focus/ocean/motion/waves1.htm.
28. Mark Hussey, *The Singing of the Real World: The Philosophy of Virginia Woolf's Fiction* (Columbus: Ohio State University Press, 1986), 7.
29. Plato, *The Republic*, Book VII, in *The Dialogues of Plato*, vol. 1, trans. B. Jowett (New York: Random House, 1937), 773–78.
30. Ibid.
31. Michel Foucault describes the shift in prevalent power structures from sovereign power with the "right of death" to biopower, "power over life," in *The History of Sexuality*, vol. 1, trans. Robert Hurley (New York: Vintage Books, 1990), 136–43.
32. Judith Butler, *Undoing Gender* (New York: Routledge, 2004), 4.

33. Ibid., 17, 4.
34. Ibid., 17.
35. Maren T. Linett, "Modernism, Feminism, and Ableism," Modernism, Feminism, and Disability Roundtable, Modern Language Association Convention, Vancouver, January 10, 2015.
36. Janet Lyon, "On the Asylum Road with Woolf and Mew," Modernism/Modernity 18, no. 3 (2012): 551–52. For a "crip theory" perspective on Lyon's essay and Woolf's complicated relationship to intellectual disability as well as neuro/affective atypicality (i.e., "mental illness," see Detloff, "Woolf and Crip Theory," in Blackwell Companion to Virginia Woolf, ed. Jessica Berman (New York: Wiley-Blackwell, in press).
37. Lee, Virginia Woolf, 184.
38. Lyon, "On the Asylum Road," 559.
39. Ibid., 569. The French from Lyon's last line comes from Baudelaire's Les Fleurs du Mal. The sentence translates roughly as "He is her brother, her likeness."
40. Virginia Woolf, Mrs. Dalloway [1925] (New York: Harcourt Brace and Company, 1981), 99; hereafter abbreviated in in-text citations as (Mrs. D).
41. Lennard J. Davis, "Constructing Normalcy: The Bell Curve, the Novel, and the Invention of the Disabled Body in the Nineteenth Century," in The Disability Studies Reader, ed. Lennard J. Davis, 2nd edn. (New York: Routledge, 2006), 4.
42. Davis, "Constructing Normalcy," 5.
43. Ibid., 8.
44. On Webb, see Davis, "Constructing Normalcy," 8.
45. Woodard, Joe. "The Disabled 'Defectives' Settle," Alberta Report/Newsmagazine 25, no. 27 (1998): 10; Douglas S. Diekema, "Involuntary Sterilization of Persons with Mental Retardation: An Ethical Analysis," Mental Retardation & Developmental Disabilities Research Reviews 9, no. 1 (2003): 22.
46. Deborah Josephson, "Oregon's Governor Apologises for forced Sterilisations," BMJ.com News Roundup, BMJ, vol. 325 (Dec. 14, 2002): 1380: www.jstor.org/stable/25453146. Accessed September 22, 2015.
47. "Alan Turing Gets Belated Apology," New Scientist 203, issue 2726 (Sept. 19, 2009): 7. Academic Search Complete, Web, July 31, 2012.
48. Lee, Virginia Woolf, 328–30.
49. Foucault, History of Sexuality, 43.

50. Rosemarie Garland Thomson, *Extraordinary Bodies: Figuring Physical Disability in American Culture and Literature* (New York: Columbia University Press, 1997), 8.
51. Woolf, *On Being Ill*, introduction by Hermione Lee (Ashfield: Paris Press, 2012), 23; Woolf, *Mrs. Dalloway*, 97.
52. Virginia Woolf, *The Years* [1937] (New York: Harcourt Brace and Company, 1965).
53. David Serlin, "Cripping Masculinity" *GLQ* 9, nos. 1–2 (2003), 159–60.
54. Robert McRuer, *Crip Theory: Cultural Signs of Queerness and Disability* (New York: New York University Press, 2006).
55. Plato, *Symposium*, trans. Robin Waterfield (New York: Oxford University Press, 1994), 49.
56. Ibid., 52.
57. Ibid., 49.
58. Woolf, *Three Guineas*, 96. On the motif of "open air," see Chapter 1.

## 4  CIVILIZATION AND BARBARISM: A REPARATIVE EXEGESIS

1. Joseph Conrad, *Heart of Darkness* (New York: Dover Publications, 1990), 45–46.
2. H. Porter Abbott, "Old Virginia and the Night Writer: The Origin of Woolf's Narrative Meander," in *Inscribing the Daily: Critical Essays on Women's Diaries*, ed. Suzanne L. Bunkers and Cynthia A. Huff (Amherst: University of Massachusetts Press, 1996), 244–45.
3. Walter Benjamin, "Theses on the Philosophy of History," in *Illuminations*, ed. Hannah Arendt, trans. Harry Zohn (New York: Schocken Books, 1968), 256.
4. Woolf, *The Years*, 337 and 339–40; *A Room of One's Own*, 52; *Orlando*, 89–90 and 108–112.
5. Virginia Woolf, "Why?" in *The Death of the Moth and Other Essays* (New York: Harcourt Brace and Company, 1970), 234. Melba Cuddy-Keane discusses the pedagogical performative aspects of the essay "Why?" in *Virginia Woolf, the Intellectual, and the Public Sphere*, 96–97.
6. Woolf, "Why?" 231.
7. Ibid.
8. Cuddy-Keane examines Woolf's early exposure to the Worker's Educational Association, with their emphasis on "dialogic" pedagogy

rather than lecturing, in *Virginia Woolf, The Intellectual, and the Public Sphere*, 89–99.

9. Eve Kosofsky Sedgwick, *Touching Feeling: Affect, Pedagogy, Performativity* (Durham: Duke University Press, 2003), 137.

10. Ibid., 126, 124.

11. Ibid., 139.

12. Ibid., 126.

13. Ibid., 124.

14. Ibid., 126, 150.

15. Brenda Silver catalogues quite a number of Virginia Woolf appearances in popular culture, some of them arguably sappy, such as the Woolf "bookmark, paperweight, fridge magnet, greeting card, and ... mug" marketed by the National Portrait Gallery, and the appearance of Woolf's portrait in an *Absolutely Fabulous* (a British sitcom). Silver, *Virginia Woolf Icon*, 278–82. I myself own a number of Virginia Woolf plush dolls and magnets (many of them, but not all, gifts from students). See, for example, the "Virginia Woolf Little Thinker" at www.philosophersguild.com/Virginia-Woolf-Little-Thinker.html.

16. Sedgwick, *Touching Feeling*, 150.

17. Ibid., 124.

18. Woolf, *Three Guineas*, 77.

19. The term is attributed to Eric Hobsbawm, qtd. in Edward W. Said, *Culture and Imperialism* (New York: Knopf Doubleday, 1993), 7.

20. On the concept of founding violence and the myth/narrative of the "foreigner" as founder, see, for example, Bonnie Honig, *Democracy and the Foreigner* (Princeton: Princeton University Press, 2001), 34–41; and Priscilla Wald, *Constituting Americans: Cultural Anxiety and Narrative Form* (Durham: Duke University Press, 1995), 257. Wald in particular draws on Ernst Renan's notion of "forgetting" as an important element of the constitution of a people ("Americans," in her analysis). Ernst Renan, "What is a Nation? Text of a conference delivered at the Sorbonne on March 11th, 1882," trans. Ethan Rundell, *Ernest Renan, Qu'est-ce qu'une nation?* (Paris, Presses-Pocket, 1992), accessed online June 16, 2015, at http://ucparis.fr/files/9313/6549/9943/What_is_a_Nation.pdf.

21. Avi Hirvonen, "The Politics of Revolt: On Benjamin's Critique of Law," *Law Critique* 22 (2011): 102.

22. Ibid.

23. Woolf, *A Room of One's Own*, 52. Cited in Jane Marcus, *Hearts of Darkness: White Women Write Race* (Piscataway: Rutgers University Press, 2004), 24.

24. Marcus, *Hearts of Darkness*, 32.
25. Caroline Bressey, "Black Londoners 1800–1900," *The Equiano Centre*, online, accessed February 5, 2015, www.ucl.ac.uk/equiano centre/Black_Londoners_1800-1900.html.
26. C. L. R. James, "The Case for West-Indian Self Government," Day to Day pamphlet no. 16, (London: Hogarth Press, 1933).
27. Parmenas Githendu Mockerie, *An African Speaks for his People* (London: Hogarth Press, 1934). Sonita Sarker remarks of British "Commonwealth" publications by the Hogarth Press, "During the period of the two Common Readers, there was one in 1929 (#192) by G.S. Dutt on Saroj Narolini (founder of the Women's Institute Movement in India) with a foreword by Indian Nobel Prize winner in Poetry, Rabindranath Tagore. After the period of the two Common Readers, in 1933, the press published C.L.R. James's *The Case for West Indian Self Government* (#322) and in 1934, Parmenas Githendu Mockerie's *An African speaks for his people* (#343)." Sonita Sarker, "Virginia Woolf in the British Commonwealth," in *Virginia Woolf and the Common(wealth) Reader*, ed. Helen Wussow and Mary Ann Gillies (Clemson: Clemson University Digital Press, 2014), 74.
28. Virginia Woolf, *Diary (1920–1924)*, vol. 2, ed. Anne Olivier Bell and Andrew McNeillie (New York: Harcourt Brace Jovanovich, 1978), p. 30.
29. Helen Carr, "Virginia Woolf, Empire, and Race," *in The Cambridge Companion to Virginia Woolf*, 2nd edn., ed. Susan Sellers (New York: Cambridge University Press, 2010), 210.
30. Murdoch, *The Sovereignty of Good*, 17. Italics in original
31. Urmila Seshagiri, "Orienting Virginia Woolf: Race, Aesthetics, and Politics in *To the Lighthouse*," *MFS Modern Fiction Studies* 50, no. 1 (Spring 2004): 58.
32. Virginia Woolf, *A Passionate Apprentice: The Early Journals 1897–1909*, ed. Mitchell A. Leaska (New York: Harcourt Brace Jovanovich, 1990), 355–56.
33. Ibid., 356.
34. Seshagiri, "Orienting Virginia Woolf," 58.
35. Jeanne Dubino," "From "Greece 1906" to "[A Dialogue upon Mount Pentelicus]": From Diary Entry to Traveler's Tale," *Virginia Woolf Miscellany* 79 (Spring 2011), 22.
36. Cuddy-Keane, "Virginia Woolf and the Public Sphere," 245.
37. Ibid.
38. Kathy Phillips, *Virginia Woolf Against Empire* (Knoxville: The University of Tennessee Press, 1994), vii.
39. Phillips, *Virginia Woolf Against Empire*, xxxv.

40. Christine Froula, *Virginia Woolf and the Bloomsbury Avant-Garde*, 1.
41. Leonard Woolf, *Barbarians at the Gate* (London: Victor Gollancz Ltd., 1939), 12.
42. Judith Butler explains the presumption (i.e., fictive production) of foundational identity thus: "The question of 'the subject' is crucial for politics, and for feminist politics in particular, because juridical subjects are invariably produced through certain exclusionary practices that do not 'show' once the juridical structure of politics has been established ... Juridical power inevitably produces that which it claims merely to represent ... Perhaps the subject, as well as the invocation of a temporal 'before,' is constituted by the law as the fictive foundation to its own claim to legitimacy." Judith Butler, *Gender Trouble: Feminism and the Subversion of Identity*, 10th Anniversary Edition (New York: Routledge, 1999), 5.
43. Leonard Woolf, *Barbarians at the Gate*, 43.
44. Ibid., 57.
45. Woolf, *Three Guineas*, 22, 64.
46. Virginia Woolf, diary entry August 15, 1924, *The Diary of Virginia Woolf*, vol. 2, ed. Anne Olivier Bell, assisted by Andrew McNeillie (New York: Harcourt Brace Jovanovich, 1978), 309.
47. Virginia Woolf, "Joseph Conrad," in *The Common Reader First Series* (New York: Harcourt Brace Jovanovich, 1953), 229.
48. Woolf, "Joseph Conrad," 234.
49. Virginia Woolf, *The Voyage Out* (New York: Harcourt Brace Jovanovich, 1948), hereafter cited in the text as (VO).
50. Phillips, *Virginia Woolf Against Empire*, 53.
51. Carey J. Snyder, *British Fiction and Cross-Cultural Encounters: Ethnographic Modernism from Wells to Woolf* (New York: Palgrave MacMillan, 2008), 98.
52. Conrad, *Heart of Darkness*, 7.
53. Woolf, *A Sketch of the Past*, 150.
54. Ibid., 152.
55. Janice Ho, *Nation and Citizenship in the Twentieth-Century British Novel* (New York: Cambridge University Press, 2015), 71.
56. Ho, *Nation and Citizenship*, 70.
57. Ibid., 67.
58. For a discussion of Woolf's references to the Armenian Genocide, see Phillips, *Virginia Woolf Against Empire*, 1–26.
59. Silver, *Virginia Woolf Icon*, 3.
60. Sedgwick, *Touching Feeling*, 146. For an extended and beautiful application of Sedgwick's reparative reading, see Robyn Wiegman's

Keynote at the Duke Feminist Theory Workshop on March 23, 2013. Available at https://trinity.duke.edu/videos/feminist-theory-robyn -wiegman. Accessed September 22, 2015.

61. Nancy Topping Bazin and Jane Hamovitt Lauter, "Virginia Woolf's Keen Sensitivity to War: Its Roots and Its Impact on Her Novels," in *Virginia Woolf and War: Fiction, Reality, and Myth*, ed. Mark Hussey (Syracuse: Syracuse University Press, 1991), 33.

62. Scarry explains, "The subject in the second half of this study is the opposite of what it was in the first half, for what will be attended to is no longer the deconstruction of the world but that world's construction and reconstruction. Thus, the particular structure of activity that will be isolated here is now not unmaking but making." Scarry, *The Body in Pain*, 161.

63. Bazin and Lauter, "Virginia Woolf's Keen Sensitivity to War," 34.

64. Jed Esty, *A Shrinking Island: Modernism and National Culture in England* (Princeton: Princeton University Press, 2004), 54.

65. Woolf, "Thoughts on Peace in an Air Raid," 243, 248.

66. Woolf, "Thoughts on Peace in an Air Raid," 245. Cuddy-Keane notes in a different context that Woolf's open or "ragged" narrative style "establishes a double textual ethics: on the part of the writer, an ethics of interpolation, in which the text is constructed as both provisional and contingent by being inserted into larger ongoing communal flow of thought; on the part of the reader, and ethics of extrapolation, in which the freedom of the future to break out into the new must do so in response to the words of the past." Melba Cuddy-Keane, "Inside and Outside the Covers: Beginnings, Endings, and Woolf's Non-Coercive Ethical Texts," in *Woolfian Boundaries: Selected Papers from the Sixteenth Annual International Conference on Virginia Woolf*, ed. Anna Burrells, Steve Ellis, Deborah Parsons, and Kathryn Simpson (Clemson: Clemson University Digital Press, 2007), 178.

67. Leonard Woolf, *Barbarians at the Gate*, 43.

68. Leonard Woolf notes that *Between the Acts* was in a near-publishable stage, "but had not been finally revised for the printer at the time of Virginia Woolf's death" (BTA 1).


## EPILOGUE   WOOLF'S LEGACY


1. Lee, *Virginia Woolf*, 753. For an extended analysis of Hare and Daldry's representation of Woolf's suicide, see Madelyn Detloff, *The*

Persistence of Modernism: Loss and Mourning in the Twentieth Century (New York: Cambridge University Press, 2009), 154–65.

2. Lee, Virginia Woolf, 744.

3. Sybil Oldfield, Research Reader at the University of Sussex and the editor of the collected condolence letters to Leonard Woolf and Vanessa Bell, notes that "The announcement in The Times on 3 April 1941, that Virginia Woolf was missing, presumed dead, and the report of the inquest three weeks later, after her body had been found in the River Ouse, coincided with the worst period of World War II for Britain. By March 1941 Czechoslovakia, Poland, Norway, Denmark, Holland, Belgium, and France had all been conquered by Nazi Germany." Sybil Oldfield, "Introduction" to Afterwords: Letters on the Death of Virginia Woolf, ed. Sybil Oldfield (New Brunswick: Rutgers University Press, 2005), xv.

4. M. Agnes Smith, Letter to Leonard Woolf, April 3, 1941, in Afterwords: Letters on the Death of Virginia Woolf, 34.

5. Virginia Woolf, "Hours in a Library," The Essays of Virginia Woolf, vol. 2 (1912–1918), ed. Andrew McNeillie (New York: Harcourt Brace Jovanovich, 1987), 55.

6. Ibid., 60.

7. Ibid.

8. Ibid.

9. Leonard Woolf, Barbarians at the Gate, 43.

10. Melba Cuddy-Keane examines Woolf's role as a public intellectual in depth, and I am indebted to her extensive work on Woolf's "pedagogy of reading," especially Woolf's distaste for lecturing and adoption of a more conversational style of teaching and learning consistent with adult education movements in early twentieth-century Britain. See Cuddy-Keane, Virginia Woolf, The Intellectual, and the Public Sphere, 86–91 and 117–22.

11. Anonymous, letter to Leonard Woolf, n.d. [presumably early April, 1941], Afterwords, ed. Oldfield, 145.

12. Virginia Woolf, "Craftsmanship," 198.

13. Woolf, "Craftsmanship," 202. On Diotima's concept of love, see Plato, Symposium, 49, and Chapter 3 in this volume.

14. Ludwig Wittgenstein, Philosophical Investigations, revised 4th edn., Trans. G. E. M. Anscombe, P. M. S. Hacker, and Joachim Schulte (Malden: Wiley Blackwell, 2009), Investigations #95–106, 243, 246, 248, 253, 258, 263, 268–69, and 293. My thanks to Gaile Pohlhaus, Jr., for her help understanding Wittgenstein's complicated and beautiful theories.

15. Woolf, "Craftsmanship," 203.
16. Virginia Woolf, "A Letter to a Young Poet," in *The Death of the Moth and Other Essays*, ed. Leonard Woolf (New York: Harcourt Brace & Company, 1970), 219.
17. Toni Morrison, "Nobel Lecture, December 7, 1993," Nobelprize.org: The Official Website of the Nobel Prize, www.nobelprize.org/nobel_prizes/literature/laureates/1993/morrison-lecture.html. Accessed September 22, 2015.
18. Ibid.
19. Ibid.
20. Ibid.
21. Smith, *Contingencies of Value*, 48.
22. Ibid., 50, italics in original.
23. Ibid., 51.
24. Virginia Woolf, "A Mark on the Wall," in *The Complete Shorter Fiction of Virginia Woolf*, 2nd edn., ed. Susan Dick (New York: Harcourt Brace Jovanovich, 1989): 83–89; Virginia Woolf, *Flush: A Biography* (New York: Harcourt, Brace and Company, 1933).
25. Hannah Arendt, *The Human Condition*, 2nd edn. (Chicago: The University of Chicago Press, 1998), 52.
26. Ibid., 25.
27. "The idea struck me: the army is the body: I am the brain. Thinking is my fighting." Virginia Woolf, Diary entry for May 15, 1940, in *The Diary of Virginia Woolf*, vol. 5 (1936–1941), ed. Anne Olivier Bell and Andrew McNeillie (New York: Harcourt Brace Jovanovich, 1984), 285.

# Works Cited

Abbott, H. Porter. "Old Virginia and the Night Writer: The Origin of Woolf's Narrative Meander." In *Inscribing the Daily: Critical Essays on Women's Diaries*, edited by Suzanne L. Bunkers and Cynthia A. Huff, 236–51. Amherst: University of Massachusetts Press, 1996.

Ahmed, Sara. *The Promise of Happiness*. Durham: Duke University Press, 2010.

"Alan Turing Gets Belated Apology." *New Scientist* 203, issue 2726 (September 19, 2009).

Annan, Noel. *Leslie Stephen: The Godless Victorian*. Chicago: The University of Chicago Press, 1984.

Antonaccio, Maria, and William Schweiker, eds. *Iris Murdoch and the Search for Human Goodness*. Chicago: The University of Chicago Press, 1996.

Arendt, Hannah. *The Human Condition*. 2nd ed. Chicago: The University of Chicago Press, 1998.

Aristotle. *Nicomachean Ethics*. Translated by W. D. Ross. 1915. In *Introduction to Aristotle*, edited by Richard McKeon, 308–543. New York: Modern Library College Editions, 1947.

Arnold, Matthew. "The Function of Criticism at the Present Time." In *The Norton Anthology of English Literature*, 7th ed., vol. 2B, edited by Carol T. Christ, 1514–28. New York: W. W. Norton, 2000.

Banfield, Ann. *The Phantom Table: Woolf, Fry, Russell and the Epistemology of Modernism*. New York: Cambridge University Press, 2000.

Bazin, Nancy Topping, and Jane Hamovitt Lauter. "Virginia Woolf's Keen Sensitivity to War: Its Roots and Its Impact on Her Novels." In *Virginia Woolf and War: Fiction, Reality, and Myth*, edited and with an introduction by Mark Hussey, 14–39. Syracuse: Syracuse University Press, 1991.

Beattie, Thomas. "Moments of Meaning Dearly Achieved: Virginia Woolf's Sense of an Ending." *MFS Modern Fiction Studies* 32, no. 4 (1986): 521–41.

Beer, Gillian. *Virginia Woolf: The Common Ground*. Ann Arbor: The University of Michigan Press, 1996.

Bell, Quentin. *Virginia Woolf: A Biography*. New York: Harcourt, Brace, Jovanovich, 1972.

Benjamin, Walter. "Theses on the Philosophy of History." In *Illuminations*, edited by Hannah Arendt, translated by Harry Zohn, 253–64. New York: Schocken Books, 1968.

Bressey, Caroline. "Black Londoners 1800–1900." *The Equiano Centre*. www.ucl .ac.uk/equianocentre/Black_Londoners_1800-1900.html. Accessed September 22, 2015.

Brontë, Charlotte. *Jane Eyre*. New York: Bantam Books, 1987.

Brown, Erica. "Introduction: Investigating the Middlebrow." *Working Papers on the Web*, vol. 11 (July 2008). http://extra.shu.ac.uk/wpw/middlebrow/index.h tml. Accessed September 22, 2015.

Brown, Paul Tolliver. "Relativity, Quantum Physics, and Consciousness in Virginia Woolf's *To the Lighthouse*. " *Journal of Modern Literature* 32, no. 3 (2009): 39–62.

Butler, Judith. "Critically Queer." *GLQ* 1, no. 1 (1993): 17–32.

*Gender Trouble: Feminism and the Subversion of Identity*. 10th anniversary edn. New York: Routledge, 1999.

*Precarious Life: The Powers of Mourning and Violence*. New York: Verso, 2004.

*Undoing Gender*. New York: Routledge, 2004.

Caramagno, Thomas. *The Flight of the Mind: Virginia Woolf's Art and Manic-Depressive Illness*. Berkeley: University of California Press, 1992.

Carr, Helen. "Virginia Woolf, Empire, and Race." In *The Cambridge Companion to Virginia Woolf*, edited by Susan Sellers. 2nd edn. 197–313. New York: Cambridge University Press, 2010.

Caughie, Pamela L. *Virginia Woolf and Postmodernism: Literature in Quest and Question of Itself*. Urbana: University of Illinois Press, 1991.

Clifford, John, and John Schlib, eds. *Making Literature Matter: An Anthology for Readers and Writers*. Boston: Bedford St. Martins, 1999.

Coffman, Chris. "Woolf's *Orlando* and the Resonances of Trans Studies." *Genders* 51 (2010). https://web.archive.org/web/20130512204349/http://www.genders .org/g51/g51_coffman.html. Accessed September 22, 2015.

Conrad, Joseph. *Heart of Darkness*. New York: Dover Publications, 1990.

Cuddy-Keane, Melba. "Inside and Outside the Covers: Beginnings, Endings, and Woolf's Non-Coercive Ethical Texts." In *Woolfian Boundaries: Selected Papers from the Sixteenth Annual International Conference on Virginia Woolf*, edited by Anna Burrells, Steve Ellis, Deborah Parsons, and Kathryn Simpson, 172–81. Clemson: Clemson University Digital Press, 2007.

"The Politics of Comic Modes in Virginia Woolf's Between the Acts." *PMLA* 105 (1990): 273–85.

"Virginia Woolf and the Public Sphere." *The Cambridge Companion to Virginia Woolf*, 2nd edn., edited by Susan Sellers, 231–49. Cambridge: Cambridge University Press, 2010.

*Virginia Woolf, the Intellectual, and the Public Sphere.* New York: Cambridge University Press, 2003.

Curd, Patricia. "Aristotelian Visions of Moral Character." In *Feminism and Ancient Philosophy*, edited by Julie K. Ward, 141–54. New York: Routledge, 1996.

Davis, Lennard J. "Constructing Normalcy: The Bell Curve, the Novel, and the Invention of the Disabled Body in the Nineteenth Century." In *The Disability Studies Reader*, edited by Lennard Davis, 3–16. 2nd edn. New York: Routledge, 2006.

Day, Dorothy. "Poverty and Precarity" The Catholic Worker 2, no. 6 (May 1952). Accessed online at The Dorothy Day Collection, June 9, 2015, http://dorothy day.catholicworker.org/articles/633.pdf.

Desalvo, Louise. *Virginia Woolf: The Impact of Childhood Sexual Abuse on Her Life and Work.* Boston: Beacon Press, 1989.

Detloff, Madelyn. *The Persistence of Modernism: Loss and Mourning in the Twentieth Century.* New York: Cambridge University Press, 2009.

"Woolf and Crip Theory." In *Blackwell Companion to Virginia Woolf*, edited by Jessica Berman. New York: Wiley-Blackwell, in press.

Diekema, Douglas S. "Involuntary Sterilization of Persons with Mental Retardation: An Ethical Analysis." *Mental Retardation and Developmental Disabilities Research Reviews* 9, no. 1 (2003): 21–26.

Dubino, Jeanne. "From 'Greece 1906' to '[A Dialogue upon Mount Pentelicus]': From Diary Entry to Traveler's Tale." *Virginia Woolf Miscellany* 79 (Spring 2011): 21–23.

Esty, Jed. *A Shrinking Island: Modernism and National Culture in England.* Princeton: Princeton University Press, 2004.

Fernald, Anne E., *Virginia Woolf, Feminism, and the Reader.* New York: Palgrave MacMillan, 2006.

Foucault, Michel. *The History of Sexuality*, vol. 1. Translated by Robert Hurley. New York: Vintage Books, 1990.

Friedman, Susan Stanford. "Spatialization, Narrative Theory, and Virginia Woolf's The Voyage Out." In *Ambiguous Discourse: Feminist Narratology and British*

*Women Writers*, edited by Kathy Mezei, 122–36. Chapel Hill: University of North Carolina Press, 1996.

Froula, Christine. "Out of the Chrysalis: Female Initiation and Female Authority in Virginia Woolf's *The Voyage Out.* " *Tulsa Studies in Women's Literature* 5, no. 1 (Spring, 1986): 63–90.

*Virginia Woolf and the Bloomsbury Avant-Garde: War, Civilization, Modernity.* New York: Columbia University Press, 2003.

Gilroy, Paul. *Postcolonial Melancholia.* New York: Columbia University Press, 2005.

Guillory, John. *Cultural Capital: The Problem of Literary Canon Formation.* Chicago: University of Chicago Press, 2013. Kindle edition.

Goldstein, Rebecca. *Plato at the Googleplex: Why Philosophy Won't Go Away.* New York: Knopf Doubleday Publishing Group, 2014. Kindle edition.

Haraway, Donna. "Situated Knowledges: The Science Question in Feminism and the Privilege of Partial Perspective." *Feminist Studies* 14, no. 3 (Autumn, 1988): 575–99.

Hare David. *The Hours.* Screenplay based on the novel by Michael Cunningham. New York: Miramax Books, 2002.

Henke, Suzette, and David Eberly, eds. *Virginia Woolf and Trauma: Embodied Texts.* New York: Pace University Press, 2007.

Henry, Holly. *Virginia Woolf and the Discourse of Science: The Aesthetics of Astronomy.* New York: Cambridge University Press, 2003.

Hirvonen, Avi. "The Politics of Revolt: On Benjamin's Critique of Law." *Law Critique* 22 (2011): 101–18.

Ho, Janice. *Nation and Citizenship in the Twentieth-Century British Novel.* New York: Cambridge University Press, 2015.

Honig, Bonnie. *Democracy and the Foreigner.* Princeton: Princeton University Press, 2001.

Horace. "The Art of Poetry." In *Horace for English Readers*, translated by E. C. Wickham, 340–63. London: Oxford University Press, 1930.

*The Hours.* Stephen Daldry, director. David Hare, screenplay. Michael Cunningham, novel. Scott Rudin/Rupert Fox Production, 2002.

Hurley, Maurice. "Q Who." *Star Trek: The Next Generation*, Directed by Rob Bowman. Gene Roddenberry, Executive Producer. 1988.

Hussey, Mark. *The Singing of the Real World: The Philosophy of Virginia Woolf's Fiction.* Columbus: Ohio State University Press, 1986.

ed. *Virginia Woolf and War: Fiction, Reality, and Myth.* Syracuse: Syracuse University Press, 1991.

Huxley, Aldous. *Brave New World*. New York: Harper Brothers, 1932.

James, C. L. R. "The Case for West-Indian Self Government." Day to Day pamphlet no. 16. London: Hogarth Press, 1933.

Josephson, Deborah. "Oregon's Governor Apologises for forced Sterilisations" BMJ.com News Roundup. *BMJ*, vol. 325 (Dec. 14, 2002): 1380. www.jstor.org/stable/25453146. Accessed September 22, 2015.

Kane, Julie. "The Varieties of Mystical Experience in the Writings of Virginia Woolf." *Twentieth Century Literature* 41, no. 4 (Winter 1995): 328–49.

Kern, Ginger. "8 Healthy Ways to Get Out of Your Own Head." *The Feel Good Lifestyle*. August 22, 2012. www.thefeelgoodlifestyle.com/8-healthy-ways-to-get-out-of-your-head.html.

King, Julia and Laila Miletic-Vejzovic, eds. *The Library of Leonard and Virginia Woolf: A Short-title Catalogue*. Pullman: Washington State University Press, 2003. http://ntserver1.wsulibs.wsu.edu/masc/onlinebooks/woolflibrary/woolflibraryonline.htm. Accessed September 22, 2015.

Koulouris, Theodore. *Hellenism and Loss in the Work of Virginia Woolf*. Burlington: Ashgate, 2011.

Lazenby, Donna J. *A Mystical Philosophy: Transcendence and Immanence in the Works of Virginia Woolf and Iris Murdoch*. London: Bloomsbury Publishing, 2014.

Leavis, Q. D. *Fiction And The Reading Public*. London: Chatto & Windus, 1939. Reprint by Read Books Ltd., 2013. Kindle edition.

Lee, Hermione. *Virginia Woolf*. New York: Random House, 1996.

Linett, Maren T. "Modernism, Feminism, and Ableism." Modernism, Feminism, and Disability Roundtable, Modern Language Association Convention, Vancouver, January 10, 2015.

Lokke, Kari Elise. "Orlando and Incandescence: Virginia Woolf's Comic Sublime," *Modern Fiction Studies* 38, no. 1 (Spring 1992): 235–52.

Lorde, Audre. "The Master's Tools will Never Dismantle the Master's House." In Sister Outsider, 110–13. Freedom: The Crossing Press, 1984.

Lyon, Janet. "On the Asylum Road with Woolf and Mew." *Modernism/Modernity* 18, no. 3 (2012): 551–74.

Marcus, Jane. *Hearts of Darkness: White Women Write Race*. Piscataway: Rutgers University Press, 2004.

*Virginia Woolf and the Languages of Patriarchy*. Bloomington: Indiana University Press, 1987.

Marcuse, Herbert. "The Ideology of Death." In *The Meaning of Death*, edited by Herman Feifel, 64–76. New York: McGraw Hill, 1959.

Martin, Kirsty. "Virginia Woolf's Happiness." *Essays in Criticism* 64, no. 4 (2014): 394–414.

McRuer, Robert. *Crip Theory: Cultural Signs of Queerness and Disability*. New York: New York University Press, 2006.

McVicker, Jeanette, and Laura Davis, eds. *Virginia Woolf and Communities: Selected Papers from the Eighth Annual Conference on Virginia Woolf*. New York: Pace University Press, 1999.

Medina, José. *The Epistemology of Resistance: Gender and Racial Oppression, Epistemic Injustice, and the Social Imagination*. New York: Oxford University Press, 2013.

Meisel, Perry. *The Absent Father: Virginia Woolf and Walter Pater*. New Haven: Yale University Press, 1980.

Micir, Melanie. "The Queer Timing of Orlando: A Biography." *Virginia Woolf Miscellany* 82 (September 2012): 11–13.

Miller John H., and Scott E. Page. *Complex Adaptive Systems: An Introduction to Computational Models of Social Life*. Princeton Studies in Complexity. Princeton: Princeton University Press, 2007.

Mockerie, Parmenas Githendu. *An African Speaks for his People*. London: Hogarth Press, 1934.

Morrison, Toni. "Nobel Lecture, December 7, 1993." Nobelprize.org: The Official Website of the Nobel Prize. www.nobelprize.org/nobel_prizes/literature/laureates/1993/morrison-lecture.html.

Murdoch, Iris. *The Sovereignty of Good*. New York: Routledge, 2001.

Nagel, Thomas. *The View from Nowhere*. New York: Oxford University Press, 1986.

Nicolson, Nigel. *Portrait of a Marriage: Vita Sackville-West and Harold Nicolson*. Chicago: The University of Chicago Press, 1998.

Office of Naval Research. "Ocean in Motion: Waves – Characteristics." *Science and Technology Focus*. Arlington. https://web.archive.org/web/20150205131240/http://www.onr.navy.mil/Focus/ocean/motion/waves1.htm. Accessed September 22, 2015.

Oldfield, Sybil, ed. *Afterwords: Letters on the Death of Virginia Woolf*. New Brunswick: Rutgers University Press, 2005.

*Oxford English Dictionary*. 2nd edn., vol. 6. Prepared by J. A. Simpson and E. S. C. Weiner. New York: Oxford University Press, 1989.

*Oxford English Dictionary*. 2nd edn., vol. 7. Prepared by J. A. Simpson and E. S. C. Weiner. New York: Oxford University Press, 1989.

Parry, Richard. "Ancient Ethical Theory." In *The Stanford Encyclopedia of Philosophy*, edited by Edward N. Zalta. Fall 2014 edition. http://plato.stan

ford.edu/archives/fall2014/entries/ethics-ancient/. Accessed September 22, 2015.

Pater, Walter. "Conclusion to *The Renaissance: Studies in Art and Poetry*." In *Selected Writings of Walter Pater*, edited by Harold Bloom, 58–63. New York: Columbia University Press, 1974.

Pew Research Center. "Younger Americans and Public Libraries." September 10, 2014. www.pewinternet.org/2014/09/10/younger-americans-and-public-librar ies/. Accessed September 22, 2015.

Phillips, Kathy. *Virginia Woolf Against Empire*. Knoxville: The University of Tennessee Press, 1994.

Plato. *The Republic*. In *The Dialogues of Plato*, vol. 1, trans. B. Jowett, 591–879. New York: Random House, 1937.

*Symposium*. Translated by Robin Waterfield. New York: Oxford University Press, 1994.

Pohlhaus, Gaile, Jr., "Relational Knowing and Epistemic Injustice: Toward a Theory of Willful Hermeneutical Ignorance." *Hypatia* 27, no. 4 (2012): 715–35.

Rabaté, Jean-Michel, ed., *A Handbook of Modernist Studies*. Hoboken: Wiley, 2013.

Randall, Bryony and Jane Goldman, eds. *Virginia Woolf in Context*. New York: Cambridge University Press, 2012.

Renan, Ernst. "What is a Nation? Text of a conference delivered at the Sorbonne on March 11th, 1882." Trans. Ethan Rundell. Ernest Renan, *Qu'est-ce qu'une nation?* Paris: Presses-Pocket, 1992. http://ucparis.fr/files/9313/6549/9943/W hat_is_a_Nation.pdf. Accessed September 22, 2015.

Rich, Adrienne. "Claiming an Education (1977)." In *On Lies, Secrets, and Silence: Selected Prose 1966–1978*. New York: W. W. Norton, 1979: 231–35.

Sagare, S. B. and Iris Murdoch. "An Interview with Iris Murdoch." *MFS Modern Fiction Studies* 47, no. 3 (Fall 2001): 696–714.

Said, Edward. *Culture and Imperialism*. New York: Knopf Doubleday Publishing Group, 1993.

Sarker, Sonita. "Virginia Woolf in the British Commonwealth." In *Virginia Woolf and the Common(wealth) Reader*, edited by Helen Wussow and Mary Ann Gillies, 65–76. Clemson: Clemson University Digital Press, 2014.

Scarry, Elaine. *The Body in Pain: The Making and Unmaking of the World*. New York: Oxford University Press, 1985.

Scott, Bonnie Kime. *In the Hollow of the Wave: Virginia Woolf and Modernist Uses of Nature*. Charlottesville: University of Virginia Press, 2012.

Scott, Charlie. "Get Out of Your Own Head: Mindful Listening for Project Managers." *SANS Institute InfoSec Reading Room*. December 19, 2010. www .sans.org/reading-room/whitepapers/leadership/head-mindful-listening-pro ject-managers-33563.

Sedgwick, Eve Kosofsky. *Touching Feeling: Affect, Pedagogy, Performativity*. Durham: Duke University Press, 2003.

Serlin, David. "Cripping Masculinity." *GLQ* 9, no. 1–2 (2003): 149–79.

Seshagiri, Urmila. "Orienting Virginia Woolf: Race, Aesthetics, and Politics in To the Lighthouse." *MFS Modern Fiction Studies* 50, no. 1 (Spring 2004): 58–84.

Silver, Brenda. *Virginia Woolf Icon*. Chicago: The University of Chicago Press, 1999.

Skelton, Anthony. "William David Ross." In *The Stanford Encyclopedia of Philosophy*, edited by Edward N. Zalta. Summer 2012 edition. http://plato.sta nford.edu/archives/sum2012/entries/william-david-ross/. Accessed September 22, 2015.

Smith, Barbara Herrnstein. *Contingencies of Value: Alternative Perspectives for Critical Theory*. Cambridge: Harvard University Press, 1988.

Snow, Nancy. "Iris Murdoch's Notion of a Loving Gaze." *The Journal of Value Inquiry* 39 (2005): 487–98.

Snyder, Cary J. *British Fiction and Cross-Cultural Encounters: Ethnographic Modernism from Wells to Woolf*. New York: Palgrave MacMillan, 2008.

Stephen, Leslie. *An Agnostic's Apology and Other Essays*. 2nd edn. New York: G. P. Putnam's Sons, 1903.

Stewart, Jim. "'Poetics … will fit me for a reviewer!' Aristotle and Woolf's Journalism." In *Virginia Woolf in Context*, edited by Bryony Randall and Jane Goldman, 322–31. New York: Cambridge University Press, 2012.

Thomson, Rosemarie Garland. *Extraordinary Bodies: Figuring Physical Disability in American Culture and Literature*. New York: Columbia University Press, 1997.

Wald, Priscilla. *Constituting Americans: Cultural Anxiety and Narrative Form*. Durham: Duke University Press, 1995.

Williams, Raymond. "Culture is Ordinary." In *Conviction*. London: Macgibbon & Key, 1958.

Wintour, Patrick. "Facebook and Bebo Risk 'Infantilising' the Human Mind." *The Guardian*, February 24, 2009. www.theguardian.com/uk/2009/feb/24/social-n etworking-site-changing-childrens-brains. Accessed September 22, 2015.

Wittgenstein, Ludwig. *Philosophical Investigations*. Revised 4th edn. Translated by G. E. M. Anscombe, P. M. S. Hacker, and Joachim Schulte. Malden: Wiley Blackwell, 2009.

Woodard, Joe. "The Disabled 'Defectives' Settle." *Alberta Report/Newsmagazine* 25, no. 27 (1998).

Woolf, Leonard. *Barbarians at the Gate*. London: Victor Gollancz Ltd., 1939.

Woolf, Virginia. *Between the Acts*. New York: Harcourt Brace Jovanovich, 1969.

"Craftsmanship." 1937. In *The Death of the Moth and Other Essays*, edited by Leonard Woolf, 198–207. New York: Harcourt, Brace & Company, 1970.

*The Diary of Virginia Woolf Vol. 2 (1920–1924)*. Edited by Anne Olivier Bell and Andrew McNeillie. New York: Harcourt Brace Jovanovich, 1978.

*The Diary of Virginia Woolf Vol. 3 (1925–1930)*. Edited by Anne Olivier Bell and Andrew McNeillie. New York: Harcourt Brace Jovanovich, 1980.

*The Diary of Virginia Woolf, Vol. 5 (1936–1941)*. Edited by Anne Olivier Bell and Andrew McNeillie. New York: Harcourt Brace Jovanovich, 1984.

*Flush: A Biography*. New York: Harcourt, Brace and Company, 1933.

"Hours in a Library." In *The Essays of Virginia Woolf Vol. 2 (1912–1918)*, edited by Andrew McNeillie, 55–61. New York: Harcourt Brace Jovanovich, 1987.

"How Should One Read a Book?" In *The Second Common Reader*, edited by Andrew McNeillie, 258–70. New York: Harcourt Brace Jovanovich, 1986.

*Jacob's Room*. New York: Harcourt Brace Jovanovich, 1950.

"Joseph Conrad." In *The Common Reader First Series*, 228–35. New York: Harcourt Brace Jovanovich, 1953.

"A Letter to a Young Poet." In *The Death of the Moth and Other Essays*, edited by Leonard Woolf, 208–26. New York: Harcourt Brace & Company, 1970.

*Letters of Leonard Woolf*. Edited by Frederic Spotts. New York: Harcourt Brace Jovanovich, 1989.

"The Mark on the Wall." In *The Complete Shorter Fiction of Virginia Woolf*, edited by Susan Dick, 2nd edn., 83–89. New York: Harcourt Brace Jovanovich, 1989.

"Middlebrow." In *The Death of the Moth and Other Essays*, edited by Leonard Woolf, 176–86. New York: Harcourt Brace and Company, 1970.

*Mrs. Dalloway*. 1925. New York: Harcourt Brace and Company, 1981.

*On Being Ill*. Introduction by Hermione Lee. Ashfield: Paris Press, 2012.

*Orlando*. Annotated and with an Introduction by Maria DiBattista. New York: Harcourt, 2006.

*A Passionate Apprentice: The Early Journals 1897–1909*. Edited by Mitchell A. Leaska. New York: Harcourt Brace Jovanovich, 1990.

*A Room of One's Own*. 1929. New York: Harcourt Brace & Company, 1981.

*A Sketch of the Past, Moments of Being*. Edited by Jeanne Schulkind. New York: Harcourt Brace and Company, 1985.

"Thoughts on Peace in an Air Raid." 1940. In *The Death of the Moth and Other Essays*, edited by Leonard Woolf, 243–48. New York: Harcourt Brace & Company, 1970.

*Three Guineas*. 1938. Annotated and introduced by Jane Marcus. New York: Harcourt Inc., 2006.

*To the Lighthouse*. Edited and annotated by Mark Hussey. New York: Harcourt, Inc., 2005.

*The Voyage Out*. New York: Harcourt Brace Jovanovich, 1948.

*The Waves*, annotated and with an introduction by Molly Hite. New York: Harcourt Inc. 2006.

"Why?" In *The Death of the Moth and Other Essays*, edited by Leonard Woolf, 227–34. New York: Harcourt Brace & Company, 1970.

*The Years*. 1937. New York: Harcourt Brace and Company, 1965.

Wordsworth, William. "Preface to *Lyrical Ballads*" (1802). In *The Norton Anthology of English Literature*, 7th edn., vol. 2A, edited by M. H. Abrams and Jack Stillinger, 239–51. New York: W. W. Norton, 2000.

Zwerdling, Alex. *Virginia Woolf and the Real World*. Berkeley: University of California Press, 1986.

# Index

Virginia Woolf's works are listed by title.